For the late Misa David who longed to see the Hajdukovic book printed in Jovo's own country: Yugoslavia.

For Diana Harper, my mentor; my husband, Reb and our children, Clint, Sarah and Ben, my parents, Hillis and Martha Eskridge and, my sister, Marian Eskridge Sexton, who all supported the goal.

For Patricia Watts, my editor at the Fairbanks Daily News-Miner Heartland Magazine, who believed and, in 1998, published eighteen biweekly installments of this story.

For my dearest friend and Belgrade researcher, Dr. Miroslav Konstantinovic who found not only the Montenegro Hajdukovics, but also Misa David. For Miro's wife, Dr. Vesna Maksimovic, and Miro's mother, Zora, who was always there. For Zorica Petrovic who taught me everything.

For Branko and Dr. Dragan Hajdukovic, Jovo's family and my Montenegrin hosts; Ilinka and Jovan Hajdukovic in Podgor-Utrg who took care of Jovo's wife and daughter.

Gratitude to Roland Thorstensson and Gunn-Britt Andersson, Rika's family in Sweden; Marie Esplund-Lynn, the Orebro Swedish archivist who translated reams of Rika's documents.

For my dear Dragan Miskovic, my graphics artist and business partner; to Filip David, Misa's brother, for his support and recommendation of Dragan Miskovic. For Majda David, my precious friend and Misa's widow.

For Charlie David, a Tetlin elder who loved John Hajdukovich.

Special thanks to: C. Michael Brown, Lael Hibshman and Irene Hansen Mead for invaluable generosity; my editors, Judi Fouse, Diana Harper and Mark Dickson.

In memory of Vuka Stepovich, John Hajdukovich's devoted fellow Montenegrin.

To the many whose lives and materials this story involved. It is an epic of the Athabaskans, John's adopted people; many Montenegrin warriors; and a Swedish farmer all in the raw country of early Alaska.

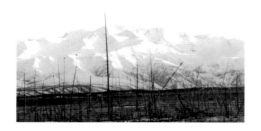

TABLE OF CONTENTS

Introduction

Born Jovo Hajdukovic ['Yo-voh 'Hi-doo-koh-vich], John Hajdukovich came from Montenegro, a land forever poor. Known as "Crna Gora" ['Sir-nuh 'Gor-uh] in the Serbian language, Montenegro, a mountain fortress, had withstood the Ottoman Empire for five hundred years. This land of rocks struck a marked parallel to Alaska, its rugged cousin across the sea.

In 1903, at the close of the Balkan Turkish Empire, John Hajdukovich crossed the sea to an untouched wilderness. He came to "The Great Land," as Alaska is frequently called, in that ephemeral time between a land's sleep and its development.

Populated by small, isolated Athabaskan bands, Alaska's Interior was a world of moose, swamp, porcupine, and glaciers. John's life became forever intertwined with these aboriginal people.

At the beginning of the twentieth century, in a frontier one-fifth the size of the entire United States, John traded from Big Delta to the Upper Tanana. He became the Natives' father, the law, and their protector. During that time, he pole-boated from the confluence of the Delta and Tanana Rivers to the Tanana's headwaters, a distance of approximately 150 miles, searching for his pot of gold.

Many aspects of Alaska's history may be traced through John's experience; specifically trading, government, business, and transportation/communication. John's life is a window into Alaska's history as it was born.

Once when asked, at age eighty-four, to point out the section lines on a map, John defied a lawyer. "Don't ask me about section lines," John snapped. "They're numbered on that map there. They're on the map, but they're not on the land. There are no marks on the land, no marks on the land. Marks there, not on the land."

John wore a little smile; he always seemed to hear a melody beyond the normal range. Trading, hunting, and mining were his excuse to ramble. Happiest when he strode across the land, John was not like other men; he was "Jovo" from Podgor-Utrg [Poh-'dgor Oo-'turg], Montenegro.

But even John needed a home. Never one to save or keep a kingdom, John depended on Rika Wallen, his friend of fifty years. Coming from her Baltic farm, Rika, a Nordic immigrant, maintained the roadhouse John had built as his home and his headquarters.

Rika came from a land that was as careful as John's was not. Her Sweden was the antithesis of John's mountain kingdom.

Like many northern trading posts, "McCarty's/Rika's Roadhouse" was situated where two rivers, the Tanana and the Delta, met. Alaska's second largest river, the Tanana, flowed from the Chisana and Nabesna rivers, from the Canadian border, northwest. From the head of the Tanana, the Indians paddled to their fishing grounds at the Tanana/Delta confluence.

After a long journey, salmon laid their delicate eggs in the back eddies of the confluence. Eagles circled the bluff picking off the decaying fish. These magnificent predators rode the wind that howled from the Alaska Range. Spinning dirt-devils whirled just above the river's sandbars. From the feet of the snow-covered mountains that lay to the south of the Tanana, a carpet of green forest paralleled the tumbling waters, rolling north.

As fall arrived, the Delta's waters slowed. Snow began dusting the dying salmon. With each day, the land and water slowly congealed into a white mass . Open springs breathed life into the cold, suspended air. Their ghostly fog drifted strangely down the breeze.

Delta, in John Hajdukovich's Serbian language, meant, "source of life." In the fertile mouth of the Delta River, fish spawned, while birds circled overhead. At the time Rika and John were born, a small band of Athabaskans were the only people who inhabited the Tanana's banks. Every fall, as the snowstorms gathered, these Athabaskans speared the dying fish for food to sustain them throughout the long winter.

Chief Isaac, 1909, Mansfield

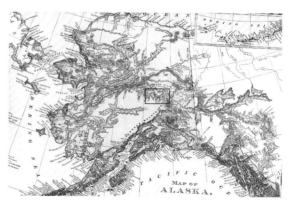

1895 Alaska map

8

Map of Montenegro/Crna Gora;
John's home of Podgor-Utrg near
Virpazar ['Veer-puhzahr] is noted

John the bear hunter,
c. 1912, Donnelly
Roadhouse, Alaska

Rika's home, Lake
Tysslinge [Tissleengih],
northwest of Orebro
[Ooruh-'broo], Sweden

Rika c.1899,
Minneapolis, Minnesota

9

Alaska: When Alaska Was a Different Land

Before "John and Rika"

Chief Healy, Healy River, Alaska, c. 1919

Long before the gold rush, Alaska was "Russian America," the czar's fur outpost. During the Russian ownership, Russians penetrated the upper Copper River area, but they did not reach as far as the Upper Tanana River.

In 1867, eight years before Rika Wallen was born, Russia sold Alaska to the United States. From 1865-1867, Explorer William H. Dall was sent by the Russian-American Telegraph Expedition to reconnoiter Alaska. In his journal, Dall wrote, "No white man has dipped his paddle into the Tanana's waters, and we only know its length and character from Indian reports."

"The Tanana," Lieutenant Frederick Schwatka, Yukon River explorer, added, "is 800-900 miles long…the largest wholly unexplored river in the world and is certainly the longest of the western continent."

After the purchase of Alaska, Lieutenant Henry T. Allen explored America's new territory. In 1885, he, and two others, snow-shoed pulling sleds from Valdez, punching through the spring's soft snow, up the Copper River valley. As the first white man to cross the Alaska Range, he gazed down onto the Tanana River valley.

Allen and his men then laced five moose skins over a spruce pole skeleton for a canoe and climbed in. The glacial Nabesna River bounced the men in their flimsy boat down the Nabesna to its confluence with the Delta River. At the mouth of the Delta, local Natives told them the river was no longer called the "Nabesna." Instead, here it was called the "Tanana."

In 1896, gold was discovered at Circle on the Yukon River. A portage was needed from the south to the gold fields. In 1898, Lieutenant Joseph C. Castner searched for the theoretical passage from the Goodpaster River to Circle on the Yukon.

As they struggled alone in sub-zero temperatures, Castner and his men almost died, beating the brush, searching for the mythical connection.

In 1898, starving and in rags, they felt forced to give up the search when suddenly they heard the noise of an ax pounding near the mouth of the Goodpaster River. Ten Native adults and six Native children were camped at the Goodpaster's mouth. The Indians fed Castner and his men, and then escorted them to the Upper Tanana River

Confluence of the Delta and Tanana Rivers, 2001; the site of McCarty's/Rika's Roadhouse is circled

where they were met by another band of Indians. "The Natives understood exactly what we needed," Castner later wrote.

Such scattered bands of Athabaskans filled the pockets of Alaska. The land's natural boundaries separated and defined their territories.

The Athabaskan people near the Canadian border were the Nabesnas. They drifted back and forth across the international border as they competed with the Canadian Athabaskans for the same caribou herd.

High in the hills separating the Copper River and Tanana valleys, the Mentasta people of the Athabaskans were a gateway dividing coastal and Interior Natives.

Downriver, following the lakes of the Upper Tanana, Natives clustered at Mansfield village and Kechumstuk [ketchumstuck] station.

Their close cousins, the Healy band, followed the caribou over the ridge tops.

Generally, the "bad waters" of the confluence of the Delta and Tanana Rivers separated the lower and upper river groups.

"The people south on the Yukon River were a generation ahead of us," Josephine Beaver of Healy Lake explained. "They were exposed to white trading posts two centuries before we were, and later, missions and schools—long before we of the Upper Tanana."

"None of us Athabaskans lived in tribes like Natives in the 'lower forty-eight states,'" Josephine said. Our people came from family clans and each one had a

11

chief. As we grouped into larger bunches, we became 'bands' led by a more powerful chief. Most of the chiefs were also medicine men.

"We were nomadic, following the game. We used wooden traps, stone axes, and lived in moss or hide houses.

"In the caribou migration corridor near Joseph village at Molly Creek, we set up drift fences. We chose an old burn and made a natural boundary with burned, stacked trees. Families made corrals, some in a series 36 miles long.

"When the caribou herds arrived, the women and children built fires pushing the animals into the open fencing. First, they allowed the leaders of the herd to slip through. After the leaders went through and the flow of animals behind them was established, the men set snares in the corral's holes to catch the followers.

"When an animal was caught, the people cut the caribou's leg tendon to hobble them. Then, they hurriedly re-set the snares.

"When they had all the animals they needed, they finished by gutting the downed caribou.

"Joseph village was the Healy band's hub. Each group had its own territory. We, the Healy people, traveled from the Gerstle River, the Johnson Rivers, the Robertson River, across Billy Creek, up to the headwaters near Joseph, on the other side of the Volkmar River, up the south fork of the Clearwater River, over to Jarvis Creek, and back down to Healy Lake."

As Josephine spoke, lake grass shimmered in the evening breeze against the setting midnight sun. Geese took wing and lifted above the mountains that surround the Healy Lake basin. A few ducks swam around the point to the old village. Mount Hajdukovich, a snowy massif named for John, towered above the Granite Mountains.

Sweeping her arm, Josephine said, "There have been people passing through, and living in, this corridor for twelve thousand years."

"The original guttural names were replaced by white missionaries, explorers, and the military. 'Mendaes Chaege Menn' [Mindez 'Ch-gh Min] became Healy Lake. Chief Geti Thege ['Gh-tee 'Th-eg] was the name of the father of Chief Healy," Josephine said as she looked off into the distance.

Continuing, she said, "All the traditions, as well as the family records, were sung at potlatches because they couldn't be written down."

"Some of my Mom's stories showed how things were back then…" Josephine searched her memory. ·

"There were twin brothers, " she remembered, "a long time ago, who were so fast, so agile that their name, 'Na teyDeh,' ['Nah 't-deh] meant 'chips exploding from a burst rock.' They could run straight up a mountainside.

"One night near George Lake, at the settlement of Ch'in Chedl Chen [Chin 'Ch-dl 'Ch-n], the Aleuts [Al-ee-'oots] (non-Athabaskan natives who live on the Aleutian chain of islands) ambushed the village. The Aleuts poised over the smoke holes of the sleeping Athabaskans' homes and filled the men full of arrows, killing most of the Athabaskan men.

"Those who escaped were ambushed outside their houses.

"The Na teyDeh grabbed their baby brother and ran. Alongside a mountain they sprinted, bouncing the baby back and forth between them as they ran across the ice. But it couldn't last; they became exhausted.

"They made a plan. If they decorated the baby with the finest beads and displayed him on the ice, the Aleuts would surely be charmed and take the baby for their own. So, they decorated the baby, and left the unsuspecting child on the ice. Then, they hurried up the mountain to sit and watch. The Aleut warriors approached. With a sweep, they sliced off the baby's head and took the beads for bounty.

"Enraged, the Na teyDeh followed the Aleuts to their homes. When they found and marked the Aleuts' home site, the Na teyDeh returned to the Interior to

Josephine Beaver, Margaret Jacob, Alice Jacob Joe,
and David Joe at Healy River, c. 1943

13

reinforce themselves with an avenging army. When they had a contingent of warriors, they headed for the Aleutian Chain. When they arrived at the Aleuts' home site, they looked down on the sleeping village from an island bluff and made a surprise attack. They spared no one.

"The chief had been in another cabin with a woman in the rear of the village. He came running out, naked and angry. The Athabaskans filled him full of arrows.

"For thousands of years," Josephine faltered, "life continued as such until 1897 when 'the world was turned upside down.'"

"The Great Death," The White Man's Gold Rush

The Year the World Was Turned Upside Down

Lieutenant Billy Mitchell cutting telegraph trail, Fort Egbert, 1903

In 1897, across America and in Europe, the economy was depressed. Shipping lines, railroads, and merchants all needed an adrenaline surge. A gold strike had been reported in 1896 by a few Alaskan prospectors. Seizing the opportunity, global businessmen started a massive public relations campaign calling the poor from the four corners of the earth: "Gold!" the cry went out. Hungry men and women responded to the frenzied campaign. The urban poor and the ill equipped, boarded trains and ships for the icy "beaches" of Skagway and Juneau.

Gold camps set up essentially over-night became hot beds of crime. To connect and to govern this chaotic "ice box," military forts were established. Forts Liscum in Valdez and Egbert on the Yukon became the points of entry into Alaska. The forts, however, were isolated and not able to connect easily with one another, or with the outside world. A message sent to Washington D.C. took a year to arrive.

14

Consequently, in 1900, Congress funded the largest construction project of its time, the Washington Alaska Military Cable and Telegraph System (WAMCATS.) Troops were sent from the "lower 48," the contiguous United States, to Alaska to cut trail for the new telegraph system. The soldiers from the temperate south were repelled by the north's hostility. They preferred the comfort of their quarters to the subarctic temperatures, and they let the project stall at

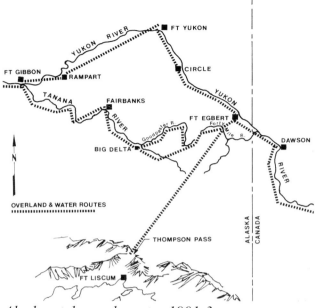

Alaskan telegraph route: 1901-3

Fort Egbert, in far eastern Alaska, not far from where they started.

Brigadier General Adolphus W. Greely, of the Signal Corps in Washington D.C., was desperate for a leader to save the project. He dispatched Lieutenant William L. "Billy" Mitchell into 1,497 miles of uncharted wilderness. Mitchell would connect Alaska with the world through the telegraph.

Before wires could be strung, however, trails had to be selected, surveyed, and cut.

To aid in the task, 150 tons of wire, food, and animal forage were shipped by steamboat to Fort Egbert. The load was then packed by horseback into the

Packhorses for the telegraph: c.1901, Eagle, Alaska

Fortymile River country to the south.

At Joseph village, Mitchell met with Chief Healy, the head of the Healy Lake Athabaskans. The Indian chief offered Mitchell a guide who, even though he was not a chief, was called "Chief" Joe. To help protect the game, Chief Healy instructed Chief Joe to guide the Army down the Goodpaster, away from a caribou migration route. Thus, Chief Healy sent Mitchell the longer way, avoiding the Fortymile caribou herd.

Mitchell trusted Chief Joe's guidance. With a string of forty packhorses, Mitchell and his men began slashing trail from Fort Egbert, through the country along the Goodpaster River, to its confluence with the middle Tanana River.

'Chief' Joe, Agnes, Alec and baby Joe
c. 1915-20, George Lake, Alaska

Lt. Mitchell established "Summit," a base at the Goodpaster's head. At the midpoint along the Goodpaster, he built "Central" station, and at the mouth, near the Native village, they constructed their main station.

Before the trail was finished, Fairbanks struck. Though Mitchell's trail was "off-limits," gold stampeders hit the trail hard. In 1902, they came sailing from the Klondike and the Yukon Rivers, down the Goodpaster, to the Tanana. Mitchell had opened the door to the "deep freeze," and the prospectors stuck their foot in.

16

Greedy prospectors swept past a people living in nomadic huts. The new culture rippled into the river valleys and over the mountains. The prospectors brought an epidemic not foreseen by the Native shaman, termed the "Great Death." They brought their technology and their pride. If the Indians were not hurt by the epidemic, they were confused and intimidated by the white man's culture.

The Indians had never heard of the Statue of Liberty, or of the promise, "Give me your tired, Your huddled masses yearning to breathe free…" But the Europeans had. Massive numbers of immigrants were streaming past the Statue of Liberty, into New York's harbor, for life's second chance.

One of those immigrants was a girl; a sixteen year old named Lovisa Erika Jakobsson, who would later be called "Rika Wallen."

Rika, fifteen years old, Orebro, Sweden

Sweden – 1875 – Lovisa Erika Jakobsson/Rika Wallen

In Sweden, taxes were high. Traditional family farms teetered on the brink of ruin. Those who lost their estates drifted to the new shoe factories in the cities. A young man, Jakob Jakobsson, believed in the land. He married a like-minded woman, Maja Stina [Mahja Stinuh]. Together, they worked hard to buy their farm. Pooling their families' resources, they bought Sodra Walla ['Soo-druh 'Val-uh], an estate near Lake Tysslingen [Tissleengih], northwest of Orebro [Ooruh-'broo], Sweden.

In 1875, the two had made a home together for seventeen years. One evening, Maja Stina was gazing out the window at the lake. The cool breezes felt good on her pregnant body. The maid entered the house bringing the evening's milk for clabbering. She waved to Maja's daughters to help. The maid poured the milk into a bowl while Christina Matilda stirred in vinegar. Maria Charlotta and Carolina Josefina dipped their fingers hungrily into the curds as the mix coagulated.

They were interrupted by their father, Jakob, returning home with their sixteen

Sodra Walla, Rika's home, Lake Tysslinge, northwest of Orebro, Sweden

year old brother, Carl. Jakob waved good-night to the three hired men, who continued on to their quarters. Jakob relaxed, sat and looked at his wife. Contentedly, he tried not to think of the two babies they had already lost. Four year old Erik ran circles around them asking when the baby would come. On April 25, 1875, Lovisa Erika Jakobsson was born, strong and healthy.

Jakob held his new daughter and said softly, "Erika," while he pondered what her future might hold. Life seemed secure, but Jakob was not sure. He gazed into the distance remembering the many who were losing their farms. Many were seeking jobs in Stockholm's new shoe factories. Would this happen to Erika…?

To protect his investments, Jakob deeded a quarter of the estate to his oldest son, Carl, while reserving a little for the other boys as well.

Life was pretty routine. The family was either working on the farm or traveling to the parish church on Sundays.

As Erika grew, her father depended on her. She was not a submissive little girl, as evidenced later in her school and church records. However, if her father gave her goats to herd, he knew the job was done. Erika loved to help him and farming came naturally to her. When forced to be inside, she submitted to learning to make goat cheese. But in the evenings, she and her sisters picked lingonberries with the new baby, Jakob, trailing behind.

When Erika was seven, she began school. At the end of every term, her school record was noted in the parish church's family archives. Perhaps due to distance, she was in school only a total of 301 days during her four years of schooling. Further, her absences were unexcused. Even with such infrequent attendance, she was an average student. According to parish records, she preferred singing to either writing or Biblical history. She was not particularly interested in church although her brother, Carl, her father, and sister, Maria, often took communion.

One particular Sunday as the family drove their buggy home from church, Jakob puzzled over news, just received. Anxiously, he rubbed his forehead as he drove the horses up to Sodra Walla. As he hung up the horses' tack, he pondered recent events. A couple of months ago, his closest friend had begged him to stand surety for his farm. Jakob, confidant of the man, had staked his own family property for that of his neighbor's. But in church, he had just learned his friend was terminally ill. Sodra Walla was vulnerable.

Outside the barn, the stately house was bustling with activity. The housemaid called, "Dinner!" as Jakob slowly walked to the house.

A few weeks later, Jakob's fears materialized. Creditors came for Sodra Walla. Already weak from work and child-bearing, the shock was too great for Maja Stina. A cancer was triggered, and at the age of fifty, she died within weeks. Ten year old Erika and her six siblings faced the world with no mother.

Following the death of his wife, Jakob moved his six, semi-orphaned children from their spacious estate into his oldest son, Carl's, small house in the brushy flats.

Living all together, the house was crowded and the family troubled. But they were not alone in their troubles. Many were losing their farms. Daily, emigrants were leaving for the United States. By spring, Carl had decided to make a new home in Minnesota.

In Minneapolis, Carl changed his last name from Jakobsson to "Wallen," coining the name from the estate they had lost, "Sodra Walla."

At home in Sweden, the lives of the remaining family continued routinely. The three sisters kept house, while fifteen-year-old Erik helped his dad, and eight-year-old Jakob herded cows.

Unfortunately, the run of tragedy was not over. Carolina Josefina, though herself still a child, became pregnant. As growing girls with no mother, Christina Matilda also got herself in trouble. She, however, opted to abort her pregnancy. Using an old Swedish method of ingesting phosphorus, Christina Matilda reached for a box of matches. Distraught, and not knowing how much was too much, she methodically ate eighty-six match heads. The combination of the pregnancy and the poison made her deathly ill. A few hours later, Christina Matilda was dead.

The situation was public knowledge; the Jakobssons were exposed to disgrace and little remained of the family's dignity. Worse, Erika had lost most of her maternal figures. Christina was dead, and Carolina's attentions were diverted as she struggled with her illegitimate baby. She could be no help to Erika. Only Maria Charlotta remained.

Erika finished school at fourteen, which was normal then for Sweden. She went to work on a neighboring farm, but any good options for her future did not exist. Returning home on the weekends, Erika listened to Maria Charlotta read Carl's letters from Minnesota. Carl described an agricultural life in the Swedish community of Minneapolis. He reported that it was not much different from home. He lived near a Lutheran church, had Swedish neighbors, but did not suffer the high taxes of home.

Carl invited the girls to join him. Ready for a move, the girls opted to accept. Erika was only sixteen, but Maria Charlotta was twenty-four. They asked a friend, Maria Eliasson, to join them as well.

March 20, 1891, Erika, Maria Charlotta, and Maria Eliasson booked passage in steerage from Goteborg, Sweden. Struggling with five bags, they boarded the Baltic trader ship, the *Rolla*. Their mattress bedrolls were crammed with clothes, dried berries, and fish, all tied securely for the voyage. They landed at Hull, England. As the ship to North America was waiting on the island's other side, they caught a train across England into crowded, crime-ridden Liverpool. They wrestled their way through the immigrants and boarded the *Arizona*. In the belly of the old clipper ship, they found three bunks. The room was filled with men, exhausted women, and screaming children from every country. Occasionally, someone made the rounds with ale.

Two weeks later, at Manhattan's Castle Garden, the girls were waiting for their passports to be stamped, to be free.

At the time that Erika (later known as Rika) arrived in the United States, there was a man still living at home in the Balkans. Far different from Rika's Baltic roots, the man, Jovo (later known as John Hajdukovich) carried rocks from his farm and pondered the blue horizon…

John's birthplace/ Milica and Andje's home, Podgor-Utrg, Montenegro, Federal Republic of Yugoslavia

Montenegro: Jovo Hajdukovic, 1879

N ear Greece, high in Montenegro's Balkan mountains, tribesmen, wailing in Arabic tones, shared their brandy as they intoned their epic stories. They sang their history accompanied by sawing a one-stringed instrument, a gusle ['goose-lay], braced against their knee. Sagas of their Kosovo roots, of tribal warriors, and of their success against the Turks and the Illyrians blazed the heavens from the mountain peaks. The "Hajduks" were highwaymen, sentries against the Turks, opportunists who waited on the road to catch strangers in their net.

Niktza Hajduka Strahinjicha [Neektzuh 'Hi-dookuh Straheenneechah] and his brothers lived in homes of stone nestled into the mountain. By day, they raided their "enemies," while their women planted gardens, carried water, and gathered firewood. In the mountains surrounding their village of Podgor-Utrg [Poh-'dgor Oo-'turg], their eagles' nest enjoyed a perfect view of Lake Skadar, bordering the country of the Illyrians, who were frequent henchmen for the Turks.

Boulders stood ready in the passes to be tripped against invaders who came from the lake or from the coast. Headhunting was fair game. On a high plateau near Lake Skadar, several severed Turkish heads were constantly on display. The lake, the largest in the Balkans, stretched across

Orthodox church and cemetery in the Hajdukovic/ Vukmanovic village, Podgor-Utrg, Montenegro, Federal Republic of Yugoslavia

21

Rade Hajdukovic,
Montenegrin Orthodox priest

country borders. Enemies slipped easily into Montenegro during the night. Although appearing peaceful, the lake sat on a cauldron separating two cultures, West and East.

In 1878, Serbia was officially liberated from the Turkish Empire. Into this focal point of the world's titans, in 1879, Jovo ['Yo-voh], or later known as "John Hajdukovich," "master guide of Alaska," was born.

On a crude bed made of spruce poles, in a one room stone house, a woman labored with her second child while Krsto [Kirsto], her husband, drank grape brandy in the animal stall under the home.

With the good news that "a son was born!" Krsto shot his gun into the air crying, "Ziveli!" [Zheevuhlee!] ("To life!") From across the trail, congratulatory shots resounded from the Vukmanovic family welcoming Jovo's birth.

During the days that followed, there was no time for Jovo's mother, Jokana [Yoh-'kan-uh], to rest. She had not only Jovo, but her daughter to care for and the home to maintain as well. Everyday, she gathered branches for cooking fuel, hauled water, and made cheese. She tended her tiny plots of hay, corn, and the vineyard. Her daughter herded the family's goats to pasture, while Krsto guarded the passes.

When Jovo was big enough, he gathered rocks to clear the family's garden. The same boulders that protected the Montenegrins also plagued them as farmers. Jovo fretted over such work. Men harvested the hay, built the houses, and guarded the passes; they did not carry rocks. But when it was time to load the family donkey to carry the summer's corn to market, Jovo was ready to go. He led the animal down the mountain to "lower" Utrg to the hydro-driven gristmill, camouflaged near the river. A widow in black guarded the mill. She put the key in the lock, and then poured the corn into the mill's hopper. Jovo rhythmically pumped the two spinning grist stones. Warm, fresh cornmeal spilled into a wooden trough, filling the air with its choking dust. When enough cornmeal was sacked, Jovo led the loaded donkey to nearby Virpazar ['Veer-puhzahr], to trade.

When Jovo was free in the evenings, he roamed the mountains in search of game. Free from chores, he invented ways to outsmart the wild pigs. His imagination never lacked.

When, on a rare occasion, his father took him to Cetinje ['Sehteen-yeh], the ancient Montenegrin capital, Jovo especially enjoyed talking with his cousin, Rade ['Rah-day], a priest. Rade was an educated man, a consulate in the court of King Nikola.

When Jovo and his father visited Rade, they hiked down the long valley to the capital. In Cetinje, foreign embassies lined the boulevard, and the city was surrounded by hills that were dominated by Mount Lovcen ['Lohv-chen], Montenegro's sentinel mountain. As Jovo walked the streets, his ears tingled with the strange sounds that poured past him: sounds of French, German, and Russian.

Rade enjoyed the precocious Jovo. When the king assigned the priest as a consulate to Saudi Arabia, he invited Jovo to accompany him. On Jovo's first trip "abroad," he ingested everything: the language..., the customs..., and particularly how the animals fared. He was surprised that in the Saudi desert even the sheep, in contrast to his own, were fat. Locals told Jovo the heavy morning dew made a rich feed for the sheep. In the years to come, as Jovo traveled further, no detail of animal life was too small, too unimportant for him to notice.

In between trips with Rade, and back home in Podgor, Jovo's thoughts were filled with all he had seen. As he again carried rocks from the vineyard, he also thought about a girl he had known all his life, the petite, pretty Vukmanovic girl. When he could, he sought her company.

But his joy was disturbed. One night while he was hunting, his mother went to the mountain's far side on her usual nightly run for firewood. As she tried to dislodge a bush, she disturbed a boulder. It rolled down on her pinning her tired body to the ground. She was hopelessly crushed, and in the morning, she was dead.

John's Courtship

Milica ['Mee-leetzuh] Vuk-manovic, whom Jovo had known all his life, had grown into a beauty. To their families' displeasure, she and Jovo spent

MiliceAndje's home after the 1952 addition, Podgor-Utrg, Montenegro

time together. Milica's family did not trust Jovo for their daughter. He had other interests; she did not. They could see that Jovo's eye was always on "the blue horizon." Years later, Jovo explained, a bit obtrusively, to his daughter, Andje ['Ahnd-jeh], "We were in love and married only because we loved each other. Because of this, Milica suffered a lot, and how it was for me, I know the best." With this, he implied he had suffered intensely, but privately.

He continued in his 1932 letter to his daughter, "Everyone was against our marrying, except Milica's mother. Milica's brother warned her, 'You will beg on the street corner if you marry that man.'" (Jovo added, "Maybe he guessed well.")

He concluded, "But we were in love."

It is possible Jovo and Milica married only for love. However, there were some whispers at the time that Milica may have been pregnant before she and Jovo married.

In those days, in the Balkans, such an indiscretion could easily result in a woman being stoned to death or banished. It is possible Jovo avoided that happening to Milica by marrying her, yet he preserved both their honor, and his freedom, by leaving everything in her name when he decided to go. It is also possible the whispers were never true.

In 1998, Jovan Hajdukovic, 72, of Podgor, remembered that after Jovo and Milica married, Jovo continued hoeing and carrying rocks out of the garden. Jovo was 25 when he suddenly threw down his hoe in disgust. He declared, "I am leaving, and I am never coming back!"

He packed his clothes, and as he left, Jovo said, "I am leaving, and I won't be back…until I have as much gold…as there are rocks in this valley!" In 1903, he followed the trail out of Podgor and hiked to the Bay of Kotor ['Koh-tohr]. He boarded a freighter there for Constantinople. As the ship pulled out, Jovo watched the land of his ancestors disappear, along with his church, his family, his wife, and his unborn child. He traveled around Greece to Byzantium to see his cousin, Archbishop Rade. From there, he began leapfrogging freighters: catching one for Egypt, and then from there, a ship to France. From LeHavre, he boarded the *S.S. La Savoie* direct to New York.

When Jovo arrived in America, he had no money. He had to earn each leg of his travel, but always his goal was Alaska: famed for its gold rush. John had friends who were already working at Juneau, Alaska's Treadwell mine.

As he worked in the new country, no one understood, or correctly pronounced, the name, Jovo. The Montenegrin name was alien to Americans and it was quickly corrupted into "John." To finish the Americanization of his name, an "h"

The Juneau, Treadwell A-J mine, Alaska-where many Slavs worked

was added to "Hajdukovic," becoming Hajdukovich. Armed with his new name and his determination, John earned his way traveling to the west coast. In Seattle, he found work "on a big railroad tunnel" before leaving, in 1904, for Alaska.

In Juneau, at the turn of the 20th century, many Croats, Serbs, and Montenegrins worked in the large Treadwell mine. Daily, many men fell to their deaths in the treacherous, deep shafts. Some bodies were sent home while others remained forever lost. John did not like underground work, and he left for Dawson, in the Yukon Territory, where he might sluice for gold above ground.

Not far behind him, John's cousin from Kolasin ['Koh-lasheen], Montenegro, Milo Hajdukovic, and Milo's boyhood friend, Ilija Milajic ['Ee-leeyah 'Meelye-eech], later known as "Charlie Miller," both arrived. These two went to work at the Treadwell, while John continued on to the Yukon. When he arrived at Dawson, all of the good ground had long since been staked for prospecting.

Deciding to move on to the next camp, John caught a steamboat, the *Cudahy*, and left, just before freeze-up, for Fairbanks, Alaska. Every day as he traveled the Yukon River, the water level dropped as more of the river froze with the cold. The steamboat grounded, unable to go further, 20 miles outside the village of Chena. John walked the rest of the way to Fairbanks: cold, wet, and tired; looking…where he might unroll his bedroll for the night.

John Hajdukovich had entered Alaska when Alaska was beginning to awaken. The door was open … and John stepped in …

McCarty's Beginnings

Lena Healy, Margaret Jacob,
Alec Joe, Abraham Luke,
1925, Healy Lake, Alaska

Soldiers/Native Village
at Goodpaster Mouth; the Rape of a Child

John entered Alaska's Interior four years after Lieutenant Billy Mitchell installed the telegraph stations. In 1901-2, Mitchell had originally built a telegraph station at the mouth of the Goodpaster River, eight miles from the Delta/Tanana confluence. The band of Indians at the Goodpaster mouth, who had helped Lieutenant Castner five years earlier, welcomed the new telegraph soldiers. The village was on the north bank of the Tanana, and the Army Signal Corps had its station on the south bank.

One night, one of the soldiers became quite drunk. He crossed the river and brutally raped an infant girl, the sister of the late Abraham Luke. Luke remembered to the day he died the screams he heard from his sister through the night. In the morning, his sister lay dead in their mother's arms.

Subsequently, the telegraph station mysteriously burned. As a result, the soldiers re-located at the confluence of the Delta and Tanana Rivers. There they built a cabin on a knoll overlooking the Tanana's south bank, a cabin large enough to be station, store, and roadhouse, the first of Big Delta.

Two years earlier, gold had been struck near Fairbanks. Re-supply points were needed all along the trail to the new camp. Ben Bennett, along with Captain Barnett, the trader and "the originator of Fairbanks," specialized in re-supplying the stampeders. Bennett sold supplies at Mitchell's Signal Corps cabin at the Delta/Tanana confluence.

In 1905, Bennett sold his inventory to Dan McCarty, a merchant, and his son, Dan Junior, a prospector. The younger Dan was involved in mining at Richardson, just north of Big Delta. Young Dan McCarty hired a "manager" to tend "Bennett's," and lavishly advertised that he had 130 tons of goods for sale at "Bennett's, ready to go."

Freeze-up, however, had kept the steamboat from arriving at Big Delta, and the supplies McCarty said were "ready to go" were actually dropped off only as far as Richardson. Anyone who wanted to purchase supplies had to go to Richardson, load the supplies they wanted, sled them from there to Big Delta, and then pay for them at Bennett's.

Soon, the ambitious McCarty drifted on to the next strike, but he left behind his name. Until well into the 1930s, "McCarty's" was synonymous with Big Delta.

Sam Abrahamson and Peter Thomas, c.1930s, Mansfield, Alaska

John's Entrance

When John arrived in Fairbanks in 1904, again he found that all the good ground was staked. He struck out for the head of the Wood River. He later wrote that he was: "… pulling a sled by the neck. Two partners were with me. We went down the Chena slough, then three miles across the portage to Clear Creek and followed it to the crossing of the Bonnefield trail."

John and seventeen other prospectors responded two years later to the 1906 strike on the Goodpaster River past McCarty's. They boarded the sternwheeler *Florence S.*, went up the braided Tanana River traveling from Fairbanks to McCarty's. From there, men used "pole boats," 24 foot, narrow craft that they propelled by shoving a long pole against the river's bottom. This was extremely difficult, going upstream, hard against the current.

27

The prospectors worked hard to penetrate the country, but they also altered the lives of the Natives who lived at the Goodpaster mouth, and at Healy Lake, competing with them for firewood and game. But there was a trade-off. The white presence brought commercial goods, finally accessible in the remote Interior.

Healy Lake; Newton, the First Trader

In 1905, William Newton, an early trader, originally of Newcastle, England,

John described his coming to Big Delta, "We arrived in Big Delta the fall of 1906. During the summer, discovery of placer gold was made on the south fork of the Goodpaster River by Alec Nichol and Tom Hendrick.

"Army Captain Beals was putting up a telegraph line that summer from Big Delta to Isabella Pass. They connected with Gulkana. We asked him if his Captain Smyth could take us with his Army freight steamer to the Goodpaster mouth. We offered him any price, 'Just make your own price,' we asked. (It's only 8 mile or a little better to the Goodpaster, but he wouldn't do it.)

"He had (to) a freight down below — on (the) Tanana River, almost to (the) Richardson. And he couldn't spare the time. And it was kinda gettin late.

("You know we landed at Big Delta on September 10, 1906.)

"We had to be on the rush. You know the Goodpaster, it can freeze, couple of cold nights. Can freeze over.

"Now, seventeen prospectors had only four poling boats and only four men to know how to pole a boat. (So we weren't sitting any too perfect.)

"Now, we have to rush it to pole it up. (There was no outboard motor.) We had to pole the boat and it was bucking the current, 3 and a half mile an hour.

("In the summer, it's 4 to 4 and a half mile an hour...Tanana River in that locality. But in the fall, it's less slow...is less current.)

"Now, all the freight, we went to unload it at the mouth of Indian village, at the Goodpaster.

("But, we had six dog teams and that saved us quite a bit of time.)

"Now, we had to still freight our dogs up the Tanana and that would take quite a bit of time.

"To save time, we put wooden runners on our sleds and took the dog teams.

"Each sled had a couple hundred pounds of flour, wrapped up in canvas on moved to the Healy River where he built the trading post, the Healy Development Company.

During the sixteen years that Newton traded, very few of the Indians spoke English. Their lives depended on game, so when famine occurred, the trading post became essential. In 1911, wildfires depleted the caribou. The crisis was further emphasized as few steamboats accessed the Upper Tanana. That winter, flour cost the Natives twenty-five dollars for one hundred pounds.

the sled. To make matters worse, we were dealing with work dogs...and they are pretty hard to handle.

"We got opposite the mouth of the Goodpaster and we waited for the pole boats. We unloaded the rest of the freight there. The boats took us across. And from there, we started up the Goodpaster.

"We dry-docked the boats and drove the dogs. We followed the Goodpaster Trail from Big Delta.

"The only traffic at that time was the natives who were using the trail, but there wasn't very many. (They had a camp at the river's mouth, and they had one 3 miles up the Goodpaster.)

"During the Fairbanks gold rush, three to four hundred people probably came down that trail during the winter of 1902 and 1903. (You know those prospectors had quite a bit of the foundation for the city of Fairbanks, too.)"

Question: "Newton was at Healy River in 1904?"

John replied, "Ah, yes."

John continued, "We stayed up the river the years of 1906-7-8. Probably thirty people used dogs, horses and mules pulling 'double enders' on the Trail from 1906-09.

"Double-enders. It's a wide sleigh, probably 3 feet wide, turned up on both ends, so if you get stuck going ahead, you can turn around, take your horse on the back end, and pull it the other way."

"You see, during the winter we had 'overflow,' so people had to go through the brush and do all kinds of hard things..."

"During the summer, people walked with a pack on their back. I walked it... lots of times."

Into this very remote setting, Newton transplanted his thirty-five year old bride, Jane Thompson. She raised their three children in this oasis as a prototype of British life in the wilderness. When Jane was not minding the store, she taught Madge, and the twins, Kathleen and Hal, with a British correspondence course. Their English was letter-perfect in an Athabaskan-only world.

William and Jane Newton's Healy River Development Company at Healy River, Alaska, c. 1917

A Fracture Between the Lower River Athabaskans and the Healy Band

"An Indian who'd learned English was 'Chief Joe,' of the lower river Natives. At the Salchaket ['Sahl-shaket] mission, he'd quickly learned English. Because he could speak English, he was asked to guide Lieutenant Billy Mitchell in making the Goodpaster telegraph corridor," explained Josephine Beaver of Healy Lake.

"But Joe was not a chief of a band at all, but only of his family clan. Mitchell simply called him 'chief' because he spoke English."

"In reality, Jarvis was the chief from 1903-14 over the Salchaket and Goodpaster/Big Delta bands, and was Joe's chief.

"About 1908, Jarvis became a Christian and began traveling up and down the river to help his people. Suddenly, however, in 1914, Jarvis disappeared. He was found drowned. Some said he was even decapitated, but certainly a bullet had been found in him.

"The tragedy was made even worse when his widow, Agnes, suddenly married 'Chief' Joe. The Salcha band, already suspicious of Joe, deeply resented it when Joe and Agnes left the band and were given protection by the Healy Lake band.

"There were whispers that 'Chief' Joe might be guilty of Jarvis' death. To this day, stress between the Salchaket and Healy bands remains," Josephine finished.

The Alaska Road Commission and the Cutoff

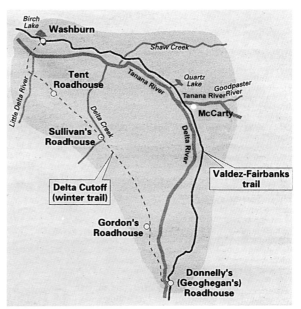

The Delta Cutoff was a detour from the Valdez-Fairbanks trail, across the Delta River, served by four roadhouses

Before there were any highways, the rivers and the Native trails were the only transportation corridors. A man could go anywhere his feet, or his boat pole would take him, albeit slowly.

With the first cry of gold in Valdez, prospectors, and then the Army, began pushing a main trail north from Valdez into the Interior. It ran up the Copper River valley, over the Alaska Range, into the Tanana valley, and on to Fairbanks.

In 1905, however, Washington D.C. wanted an "all weather road" from Valdez to Fairbanks. The Alaska Road Commission was created to construct the "road." In Washington D.C., "a road for all seasons" through the Alaskan Bush seemed like "a reasonable idea."

The new A.R.C. decided to shorten the existing trail and make it more efficient. The "shortcut" would leave the established trail at Donnelly Roadhouse, just south of Donnelly Dome, cross the river from east to west, travel through the foothills and flats, pass back over the river ice, west to east, and emerge twenty miles north of Big Delta at Richardson, thereby deleting 35 miles.

A strong argument for the detour was to find a route protected from the high winds and whiteouts north of the Alaska Range. However, the new route would require, not one, but two river crossings (the Delta and the Tanana): very tricky for freight horses. Once across the river, the Cutoff's steep grades proved to be icy for freighters hauling uphill. Even worse, in summer, the trail sank into a swamp. In the end, the Cutoff was no "all weather" road at all.

However, probably because the federal government had sponsored the road's

31

creation, two federal agencies, the Alaska Road Commission and the U.S. Postal Service, pressed hard for, and gained, the detour. Independent freighters, however, generally avoided the Cutoff. Finally, in 1909, the A.R.C. installed a government ferry at McCarty's Tanana crossing, causing the original Valdez-Fairbanks route to once again become the favored trail.

In the winter only, the Valdez-Fairbanks northbound traffic crossed the mouth of the frozen Delta River at McCarty's and connected to the Cutoff trail. They continued traveling north to Washburn. Travelers emerged at Washburn, the last stop, before the final Tanana River crossing.

By 1920, the Cutoff was no longer used, and certainly, by 1923, when the railroad was completed from Anchorage to Nenana, it was discontinued.

McCarty

McCarty's original roadhouse with telegraph operator, and possibly, Al Maxey, c.1914

South of the Granites, Mount Hajdukovich is a reminder of John Hajdukovich, the man who searched the hills for his rainbow and its pot of gold. By 1906, John's cousin, Milo, had joined his distant cousin, John, in Big Delta. The "Hajdukovich brothers," as they were called, searched for color up Jarvis Creek, and tried, by some "Montenegrin alchemy," to convert the rocks into gold. By 1909, however, their prospect holes had become hopelessly flooded.

Needing something reliable, Milo got a job cutting telegraph trail from Big Delta to Isabel Pass. In 1910, using his profits, he started a fox farm. Around that time, he and John began headquartering at Big Delta.

"The first time," John said, "I entered the McCarty Roadhouse was in 1906 … I was twenty-six years old. That little building was the first trading post, roadhouse, post office, and telegraph station, all rolled into one. Everything centered in that little building. Everybody helped each other." To cross the Tanana River, all a person had to do was to holler from one side of the river, "Bring the boat over!" and someone would come.

In 1909, however, the government ferry was installed. Two forty foot towers were driven into either side of the Tanana, and these were connected by a cable strung across the river. A guide wire, hanging down from the cable, was attached to the ferry. As the ferry launched to cross the river, the current caught the ferry's angled rudder and pushed the boat through the water, like the wind hitting a sail.

Former roadhouse owner, Dan McCarty, had drifted with the gold strikes. A homesteader, Alonzo Maxey, began running McCarty's abandoned inn, while John or Milo operated the new government ferry. During the winter, when the ferry was dry-docked due to freeze-up, John hand-cranked a cable chair across the open water.

"Butch" (Henry) Stock

"Butch," a close friend of John's, earned his nickname by herding cattle to Dawson. He was reputed to have once been one of the Klondike's richest men. But Butch had speculated on claims, buying them sight unseen, and he was soon broke. Rich or poor, it was the same to Butch. He was often seen walking with his dog, blithely ignoring the rainwater running out of his toeless shoes.

"Butch," Ted Lowell remembered, "was a

James Geoghegan, Jack Singleton, Meyers, John Hajdukovich at Riley Creek hunting camp, 1912

33

Jim Thompson and "Butch" Stock

man who'd give anybody the dirty shirt off his back." He frequently offered his guests pancakes made from the sourdough batter stored under his bed. If a mouse's tail was sticking out of the bowl, he simply tossed it out and whipped up the hotcakes, all the same.

Butch was John's favorite hunting partner. The two of them hunted on upper Jarvis and Riley Creeks for the Fairbanks' meat market, and then, rafted moose, sheep, and bear meat up north to Fairbanks to sell. At McCarty, they sold wild sheep meat to the U.S. Army Signal Corps.

Butch had three places: a cabin just upstream from McCarty's/Rika's Roadhouse, one across the Delta, and a third near the Alaska range. His favorite place for hunting was near Donnelly Dome at Beal's Cache. On a Dall sheep trail, Butch had a "dugout," with a trapdoor near a salt lick. In the evening, when the animals began to nibble pea-vine, Butch simply slid his rifle out the dugout's trapdoor, and "popped" a sheep.

In his buckboard, Butch hauled the game to a root cellar upstream from his Big Delta cabin. The root cellar, a seventy-five foot tunnel, was loaded every spring with ice packed into the walls. Meat and vegetables could be preserved for a season. During the winter, the deep earth protected the stored vegetables from temperatures that reached -50° F.

John on right, clowning, in 1912, with grizzly sow and cub skull and hides

34

Dr. Meyer, John Hajdukovich on right, caribou hunting in 1912

The cellar tunnel fronted on both the river and the trail. John could unload his supplies directly from the boat into the root cellar.

Upstream, there were two other bachelor cabins near Butch's. When John was asked who else lived at McCarty's, he replied, "Theodore Crowson, Art Wheeler, ah, 'Butsch' had a place."

John said the Goodpaster Trail was used by "three hundred natives and seventy-five whites. These people was traveling," he said, "most of them, up the Richardson Highway, south, and to the Upper Tanana."

When John was asked how many guests stayed per night in the small McCarty's cabin, he replied, "When the ice would support… fifty-four one night, they was laying like, uh, sardines all over the floor.

"Have a plenty a blankets and canvas. Everybody was happy.

"Lots of fire, kept em warm."

(Some of these were traveling south down the Valdez-Fairbanks Trail; some were going up the Tanana, prospecting…)

One of the prospectors, for whom McCarty Roadhouse was named, was involved in scandal: young Dan McCarty. In 1919, the *Fairbanks Daily News-Miner* reported that McCarty, a carouser, had apparently enraged his wife, "Laughin' Annie," more than once, and neither of them was laughing anymore. Annie grabbed her husband's gun and "gut shot" him. All night, McCarty suffered a slow death. However, he did not blame his wife, but he did say, "she done a bum job on me."

Sugar Beets and Rationing/McCarty Agriculture

Big Delta's McCarty's Roadhouse was a hub, an oasis serving the wilderness. All food either had to be either shot or raised. Once, John shared a story about sugar rationing and farming on the banks of the Tanana between 1906-1915. The first farmer, John said, was Theodore Crowson.

John: "Yes. Theodore Crowson. He had to till and clear the land, and he raised everything he needed for himself. Even grow sugar beets, made a sugar out a them. He was living off the country. He raised everything he needed. He used it until 1918.

"In 1918, Judge Griffin, United States commissioner from Richardson, come up to Big Delta. To check up how much sugar we had" (...during World War I's sugar rationing).

"Even I had a cache there. Lots a sugar there. I showed it to him.

"He took inventory. And he told us how much we could use.

"I took the gold scale and put my allowance on the scale. It was enough for one

McCarty's roadhouse built 1914

meal, so I told him, 'I'll tell you what I'll do; I'll never touch the sugar till war is over,' and I never did.

"But Theodore…wasn't like that.

"'But,' he says, 'you don't have to check on my sugar.'

"'How's that?' the Judge asks.

"'I got all the sugar I want. Well, after all, it's a sugar beets.'"

John continued his history, "And I farm…on the land that used to belong to Al Maxey. That land was turned over to the public domain.

"Land office wrote to me and asked me about if I want to stake a claim there.

"I came to Fairbanks and said, 'I don't want no homestead, but I would like to farm there for few years. Just for experiment. But,' I said, 'if anyone wants to stake for a homestead there, I'll move that place.'

"I was farming. Just for experiment. Used to raise 2-3 ton of potatoes, 2-3 ton of turnips, and the rest sold by the pound, give it away … and, I couldn't get rid of it … I put it in a big root cellar that was a T-shaped tunnel, going 75 feet one way … and 75 feet the other with double, insulated wooden doors. We stored vegetables in a sandbags."

Alonzo Maxey and the U. S. Army Military Reservation

Alonzo Maxey, was a dried up little man of whom John was very fond," recalled Ted Lowell. He was one of the first homesteaders. From the beginning, Maxey stirred things up. First, he accused Bennett, the original owner of the roadhouse, of trespassing his property lines, and then, the U.S. Army.

Maxey watched the behavior of the telegraph operators closely. He filed complaints accusing the U.S. Signal Corps soldiers of "immoral behavior" and also cited "misuse of government property." He protested everything: the soldiers, the meat market hunters, and trespass of his homestead's borders.

Until 1912, Maxey charged the U.S. Army rent for the three acres of his homestead they used.

John, who frequently negotiated for Maxey, pointed to the map, explaining the story, "This is McCarthy military reservation, located at Big Delta, about a mile or so from the Tanana river bridge. Used to be Al Maxey's corner post right here.

"The telegraph station was a little over 3 acres and was surrounded by [what

McCarty ferry; original McCarty roadhouse far left; Signal Corps telegraph buildings, c 1912

would become] Rika Wallen's homestead. The station was about 70 feet or so from Rika's and was leased from Al Maxey in 1906."

"This was Al Maxey's homestead: 320 acres. Only he had it staked under the wrong homestead law. His contract said the army would lease it for twenty years, for a one dollar a year. That's pretty long.

"At the end of twenty years, the Army was supposed to turn the land back to Maxey with all the improvements. (Unless, it was some new arrangements made.) They rented it until 1912.

"That is, in 1911, some friction developed between Maxey and the soldiers. A lieutenant in the Army came from Valdez to check on us there.

"And he was mad, annoyed that there was trouble between Maxey and the Army, that either party would interfere with the other, you know …

"Somehow, someway, the Army got into Maxey's business … so the friction was critical … The conflict got worse and they couldn't agree with Maxey … so the lieutenant ordered his men to stake the ground. They did.

John and Butch pole boating a dog sled across the Tanana, c. 1917

*The Signal Corps buildings; the General Jacobs steamboat;
the ARC ferry, c.1910*

"Then, Maxey couldn't take the matter to court, cause he didn't have the money. He was broke. (He wanted to include that staked military ground in his homestead, but the Army had already withdrawn it for military purposes...) He wanted to include that 3 acres in his homestead. He already thought it was.

"In 1912, President Taft signed the military reservation into existence.

"Now, the reservation's right there." After the U.S. Supreme Court ruled against Maxey, he left the roadhouse to John. Maxey wanted a fresh start and moved across the Delta River to build another "roadhouse." However, the fight had taken most of Maxey's strength. In 1913, he was declared insane in Mount Tabor asylum, and two years later, he died in the state of Washington.

For seventy-four years, the military's 3 acres remained a federal island in the midst of the roadhouse's homestead, mostly forgotten.

The Treacherous Tanana

McCarty's was the head of commercial freighting for the area, the relay for the Upper Tanana. Once, when a light draft steamboat left Fairbanks for the Upper Tanana, they reported it was a nightmare: "Due to a 10 mph current, 30 to 40 channels, and 123,456 turns, we progressed only a half mile in an hour.

"On a 175 mile trip, the boat's wheel traveled 1052 miles.

"Low water, tortuous braids, and no viable shoreline caused the trip to be abandoned." The party had to walk the rest of the way.

The military developed a special light-draft steamboat, the *General Jacobs*, but even so, trips were made only during July's high water.

Fraternity of Prospectors...

Alaska was built by prospectors. They worked like dogs, looking for a supportive industry, while leaning on their shovel waiting for word of the next strike. Statehood, they thought, was what they needed, and they hoped Alaska's first U.S. District Court Judge James Wickersham might help obtain it.

John recalled his comrades of those early days. He remembered, "We had around eighteen to twenty prospectors, between 1906-1915, who headquartered at Big Delta. They used to meet every fall for a couple of days and then again every spring for two or three days.

"Now in the spring, as soon as the ice was out of the river, they floated down the river on the rafts or in the boats. They all waited until everybody got there. Everybody.

"That was the only couple of days of vacation we had.

"We had only three cabins, and stayed a couple of days.

"Now each cabin was lined up with bunks: three high, lots of room for everybody. Only we couldn't cook inside of the cabin. No room. Had to cook outside.

"After that in the spring of the year, the prospectors scattered, everyone in his own direction. Most of them went to Fairbanks to work for the summer.

Chief Joe, Josh "Jack" Ray, Chief John Healy, John Hajdukovich
at Healy River cabin, c.1920

"I stayed at Big Delta.

"In the fall of the year, they got back together and followed the Goodpaster Trail. All of them were poling their boats up the Tanana.

"They made discoveries on the Upper Tanana…from Richardson Highway to the border: 200 miles — all the drainages from the Yukon River to the Alaska Range.

"There in the mountains, I took a small hydraulic plant to McCumber Creek in 1911. Every year, I got enough for a grubstake.

"But in 1913, there was the discovery of gold in Canyon Creek. (The discovery was made in the spring of 1907, but) — In 1913, they did more work, and they made a trail, so we rushed in.

Ted Smith, builder of McCarty's/Rika's Roadhouse at Clearwater Creek, 1927

"At Clearwater Creek, we built a big raft and we drove our horses across on the raft. (It's not very wide stream…) We took them across. Then we moved our freight up to Healy River, over to Healy Lake, and on beyond to Canyon Creek."

"The stampede was fifty to sixty people from Big Delta.

"With a horse, I moved a 'steamin Jenny,' a steam boiler. I did a little mining in a big way. Each one of the prospectors brought a dog sled and 'outfit.'

"Emil Hammer was the main discoverer. Captain Morgan, a steamboat captain, worked the ground 3000 feet above me.

"For two years at Canyon Creek strike, we worked, but only struck oil, oil and water. When we hit water, that was the end of the mining."

The Last International Gold Stampede at Chisana

In a 1911 *Fairbanks Daily Times,* Captain Northway was quoted as saying, "If ever a prospector had a paradise, the Upper Tanana is it." The cry, "Four penny weight (equivalent to $3.20) on the end of the shovel!" was a language all prospectors understood.

By 1913, they came running from all over the world. In a global advertising campaign, the public relations magnates advertised the Tanana as "navigable." Stampeders from many countries pushed up the narrow, twisted channel, searching for the remote Chisana River. They winched their boats up the river by cabling the boats to shallow-rooted trees. When the trunks snapped, the boats were sucked into the fast current and filled with water, gone forever.

The prospectors pushed deep into the Nuzotin Mountains in eastern Alaska. Overnight, deserted valleys became cities of hundreds, complete with a dentist.

Harry Blake, the first to report on Chisana, wrote to his partner, Charles Span, at Chicken, on July 5, 1913, saying, "I advise you to come over our old trail as soon as you can get away. We have hit it very good.

"I have your rifle, robe, your two dogs. I will pole grub up to Mosquito forks, then pack it over Old Man and Old Woman mountains.

"If you come, don't bring grub, but come with a 'thirty days' pack on your back, same as we did in 1902.

"These pay creeks will leave Dawson in the dust…We have gold on six different creeks now.

"Blackie just said he hit it on Pine creek.

"Well, Charlie, come and be damn quick about it. From your old friend, Blake.

"P.S. You will find me at Pine, Eldorado or Moose creeks.

"Four pennyweight on the point of the shovel. Good-bye."

A year later, Chisana was summed up by the prospectors as, "One dismal failure."

When asked if he participated in the Chisana strike, John replied, "Oh no, I was at Big Delta in 1913. But," he added, "there were probably eighteen hundred there, maybe more. I never thought to keep track of that.

"Sometime I used to take fifty of them on the scow. I'd have to leave half of them, but I'd take the other half.

"Those walking followed the Richardson Highway up to Summit Lake and then after the Alaska Range, they continued south. They crossed where the Nabesna Mine road is now…and then, followed the black hills to Chisana."

The thousands of white men traveling the Native trails, however, left more of a lasting impact on the land, and on the Native people, than any gold ever discovered. In the Healy River strike alone, fifty to sixty white men forever changed the Healy Lake Natives.

Chief Healy watched the white men strip the hills of firewood as they directly competed with the Indians for cabin logs, game, and fur. Worse, the chief fought the trend as some of the Native women became involved with the white bachelors. Annie, a once beautiful woman, was ostracized by the chief for her philandering. Annie greatly aged after ten years of such stress.

The chief could see what was coming …

42

Once when he was at his remote camp up the headwaters of Healy Lake, a white man appeared, "necking a load" (pulling it from his head). Healy, greatly frustrated, complained to a friend, "White man is coming." Powerless to change destiny, the chief said he had wanted his sons to replace him, but felt they too … were becoming white men. Sighing in futility, the chief said, "I'm old man, medicine man."

Even his name did not remain untouched. Two prospectors, Pat Doherty and Josh Ray, could not pronounce his Indian name and began tagging him with a nickname, "Healy." The chief with his whiskered, iron gaze reminded them of North American Trading and Transportation Company head, John Jerome Healy, also a man with a goatee and focused expression. The nickname stuck.

Chief Healy, who resisted the white flood, was caught in it. His real name was forgotten, his family's name, and that of the lake were forever lost to history.

Similarly, when Captain Northway made an historic trip to the Upper Tanana, he met Chief T'aaiy Ta' [Tah-ee 'tuh]. Apparently "deciding to adopt him," the captain renamed the chief after himself, "Northway." The chief, his family and their village subsequently lost their original name, and like the Healy band, all the Nabesna groups became known not by their Indian names, but as "Northway."

The Building of the Roadhouse

The stampeding masses to Chisana caused John to realize that a larger roadhouse was needed, and because it was located on the Valdez-Fairbanks trail, John knew the need would only grow. John also wanted his wife and daughter to join him in Alaska, so he was also thinking of making a home. He contacted Charlie Maxfield, and his partner, Ted Smith, builders of the Clearwater Creek lodge. John asked them to build his new roadhouse.

By the spring of 1914, Maxfield was floating trees to the site, and rolling them up the McCarty (south) bank. He notched the round, irregular logs into a large two-story structure.

When it was finished, John's business style was to ask guests to "be at home," and leave some money on the table. It was a traditional method, and the stationary aspect of running a roadhouse did not interest him.

John described, "I bought Al Maxey's roadhouse in 1913. The next year I built a new roadhouse. Part of the house is there now … I ran it until 1918." The handsome building, with its windows all framed in white, sat on the south bank

McCarty's Roadhouse, c.1922

of the Tanana River, complete with a ferry. The roadhouse stood ready for the occasional steamboat traffic and for those traveling the trail.

In 1932, John wrote the following to his daughter on the back of a photo of the roadhouse, "This is the house where I wanted to bring you and live together as a family …" But Milica, John's wife, refused to come. Years later John said, in a ponderously heavy tone, "I sold that roadhouse, yes … to Rika Wallen"…

The Family Left Behind;
MiliceAndje and the Roadhouse

On John's 1916 application papers for citizenship, he wrote that he was married to Milica, and had one child, Andjelina [Ahnd-juh-lee-na], born September 1903. In the Montenegrin understanding, the two women would always belong to John: "Jovovo," ['Yo-vovoh] as they were called in Serbian, meant "belonging to Jovo."

Motivated by poverty, Balkan men often went to "Amerika," but usually they returned home, if not in mid-life, then in death. Even those who died in the Juneau mine were ultimately returned to Serbia. All the Hajdukovics were buried in the cemetery surrounding Podgor's ancient Montenegrin Orthodox church.

When World War I began in 1914, Milica was thirty-four and Andje, only eleven. Andje was crippled, but still tended the village's goat herd. They were supported, in part, by the family who surrounded them, Milica's Vukmanovic relatives, and John's Hajdukovic relatives.

John's failure to return, his lack of support, and lack of communication damaged his reputation in a country where pride is everything. His name brought not honor, but infamy. Worse, communication between John and his family was impossible during World War I. Montenegro was decimated as they defended the Serbs and fought against the Austro-Hungarians and Bulgarians. A Hapsburg headquarters was in the village next to John's home, Podgor. Those considered not loyal to the Austro-Hungarian occupiers were sent from the villages to concentration camps in Bosnia.

After the war, those who survived suffered famine, disease, and deep poverty. Weakened and disunited, the tiny kingdom of Montenegro was swept into the Kingdom of Serbs, Croats, and Slovenes, resulting in the "first Yugoslavia."

John followed all these events closely by reading the news from the home front in Chicago's oldest Serb newspaper, *Serbian Unity*.

The global chasm further separated John from his roots and only deepened his natural solitude. The Athabaskans, also children and strangers on this earth, became John's adopted people. For them, he ultimately lost this world's goods.

Goatherder, Podgor-Utrg, Montenegro, FRY, 2001

45

Prospectors Scattered to the Four Winds

L-R: John and Joe Joseph, Judge Wickersham, & Old Seline at the Salcha, c. 1905

Before World War I, John had enjoyed the small fraternity of prospectors. They had lingered waiting for statehood, thinking it would bring the support structure necessary for an expedient mining industry. Chisana had been the frontier's finale, before the madness for gold was replaced with global insanity.

John described the war's effect on an innocent time, before the prospectors were scattered to the four winds.

John: "In 1915, Judge Wickersham was a forced to introduce a bill in Congress to provide for a statehood for Alaska.

"And you know, we expected to get it through that time. In both 1915 and 1959, the Judge was for statehood. He said, 'I don't care what anybody says … We have a lot of young men here: miners and prospectors, with a great interest in mining/prospecting.'

"When the Judge returned from Washington D.C., he said, 'Well, we didn't get the statehood, but we got to work for it. Fight for it until we do get it, get a 'godfather."

"Then some of the boys asked him, 'Just how long do you think? We are afraid…?'

"'I'm afraid,' he says, 'that we will have to wait forty years.'

"John added, 'We waited forty-five.'

"Then some of the prospectors in 1915 said, 'What's the use to wait? Forty years from now, we old man. What is good to me?'

"Okay, then … they left.

"Some joined English Army, and some joined Canadian Army.

"You know, they went to old country to fight the Kaiser: first World War.

"And the rest left Alaska for higher wages. Then … our country got into war. They joined our Army. A good many got killed.

"Those who left--they didn't return.

"That was a great of financial loss. All our mineral prospects laying there, been laying there for forty years right now.

"After the war, we considered the situation again … Every few years, we reviewed what can be done … But it remained just the same, with no change."

However, change came as the modern age and its machinery were ushered in at the war's end. While the mud trail from Valdez to Fairbanks was spliced with unbridged creeks, Bobby Sheldon dared to purchase one of the first automobiles, a 1906 Pope Toledo.

Beginning in 1913, Sheldon repeatedly drove the double seater over the mountains, through the streams, across the swamps, back and forth from Valdez to Fairbanks. He hauled passengers through the Interior with the first taxi service.

There was, however, the understanding that when his taxi came to a hill, everyone jumped out, gave it a boost, and hopped back in as they descended the far side. It is most likely Rika entered the Alaskan Interior in Bobby Sheldon's taxi service.

Standing: Bobby Sheldon & his Pope Toledo automobile.
Front seat: R-L: Wilbur, Walter Jewell. Rear seat:L-R: Wilma Carlson,
Mrs. Jewell, Mrs Hal Bailey, Mrs. Henry Wood, 1909, Fairbanks, Alaska

Rika's Entrance

Mrs. Mary Hellsten née Maria Charlotta Jakobsson, Minneapolis, c. 1899

From the U.S. immigration portal in 1891, Erika and her sister received their visas and ran to catch the Minnesota-bound train for Minneapolis. Their brother, Carl, was waiting for them in the small, agricultural community. Soon, their other brother, Erik, would also join them. Carl had a nice farmhouse and a small herd of cattle. He needed some help.

Not long after Erik arrived, the Jakobsson brothers and sisters celebrated by going to a photography studio. In a lavish session, each of them posed in costumes more elegant than their life really supported.

During the ensuing nine years that Erika lived in Minnesota, Carl married and had four sons and one daughter. Maria Charlotta married a Mr. Hellsten. Their brother, Erik, who never cared much for farming, disappeared one day leaving no trace of his whereabouts. What happened to Erik no one really knows. He never cared about agriculture while Carl, on the other hand, was a farmer and enjoyed his home and family.

One day after a particularly hard rain, two of Carl's sons were playing near a swollen river, and before anyone realized it, they lost their footing and fell in. Carl, who was quite close, jumped in after them. But it was useless in the torrent. All three of them drowned in the raging river. Now all that remained of the once large family were Carl's widow and the remaining three children.

When Erika was twenty four and Maria Charlotta, thirty three, they received word their father had died in Sweden. It seemed time to move on. In 1899, Erika, along with Maria and her husband, Mr. Hellsten, left the Swedish community for the frontier city: San Francisco.

In Oakland, California, the Hellstens made a home, while Erika found work cooking for the wealthy Hills Brothers Coffee family. As Erika got comfortable with the estate's staff, they affectionately shortened her name to "Rika."

As time passed, the Hills Brothers family became so fond of Rika that they gave her some lucrative property near what would become the Oakland bridge.

However, when the 1906 earthquake destroyed much of San Francisco, the wealthy were also leveled. In Alaska, years later, Rika recited stories of what it was like to be caught in fire, in darkness, and shaking. Much of San Francisco's economy was destroyed. Recovery was slow. Even eight years later, the news of Alaska's Chisana gold rush of 1914 offered hope to those struggling with destroyed lives.

Carl Wallen (born Carl Jakobsson), Minneapolis, c.1899

Rika, who was without a job, heard that work was plentiful in the northern gold camps. She longed for a home like Sodra Walla, the one she had lost. She felt Alaska, particularly, would be like Sweden. In 1916, Rika took a chance and booked passage for Valdez, Alaska. At the age of forty-two, she left California attempting to find what she had lost in childhood.

In Valdez, Rika rode with Bobby Sheldon's taxi service as far as the Kennicott copper mine. There, she got a job cooking for a mining crew. When the season was over in mid-October, she left by horse sleigh, her feet covered in brick-

Stage sled at entrance to Keystone Canyon, Valdez-Fairbanks Trail, c.1907

warmed blankets. The ride to Fairbanks cost one hundred fifty dollars and took a week.

Rika's clothes, however, were not suitable for the exposure. Her clothes were those of the city, and her feet were clad only in leather shoes. Moving across Alaska at a snail's pace, while sitting all day with no protection, became grueling. At each day's end, she dragged her frozen, stiff body into the primitive roadhouses. Inside, the travelers competed for the few bunks made of spruce poles, called "pole bunks."

On the fourth day, as the sleigh crawled against the howling wind through the mountain pass, Rika vowed she would winter at the next roadhouse, no matter what it looked like.

North of McCallum and Phelan Creeks, Rika saw what appeared as "a castle," Yost's roadhouse, in the Alaska Range. The short buildings were built "shotgun" style, one behind the other. As Rika approached, smoke curled from the roof's tin smokestack; the glow of a kerosene lantern warmed the view from the low windows. Rika inquired within if Yost needed a cook. When he nodded, she swore she would never leave until spring arrived.

During the nights of that long winter, Rika listened to the wind howling through the range. Near the roadhouse, blizzards often swept across the long, frozen lake. Like a lighthouse, the dinging of a bell near the roadhouse guided sleighs across the deep dark of the endless lake.

For seven months, Rika listened to the "ghostly," haunting sound of the bell. During the long black nights, alone with a kerosene lamp, Rika longed for spring.

In June, she caught Bobby Sheldon's first taxi ride and drove the raw trail north to Fairbanks.

Friss' Lodging,
a Boarding House on Front Street

It did not take Rika, a woman and an accomplished cook, long to find a job in Fairbanks. A boarding house, which offered "two dollar lodging weekly for a single room with spring beds," advertised needing a baker. In the spring of 1917, a pretty, Swedish baker began cooking for the prospectors of Fairbanks.

John was also eager to go prospecting. His cousin, Milo, had just announced to Fairbanks that gold had been found on Michigan Creek off the Goodpaster River. Ready to go, John needed someone dependable to run his new roadhouse.

Described as "high, wide and handsome," John, a gentleman, approached Rika several times at the boarding house. He pointed out, in his charismatic way, the strategic location of the roadhouse, and asked if she might consider cooking for him. Rika, who had fed the miners at Kennicott and the stage passengers at Yost's, was equal to the task of the McCarty oasis at Big Delta. John explained that because Big Delta was a midpoint on the way from Fairbanks to Valdez, the portal to Alaska, McCarty was sure to grow. Rika finally agreed to travel to the remote hostelry and try it for a winter.

When "Butch" Stock heard that a woman was cooking at McCarty's, he hitched up his buckboard to see for himself. Upon his arrival, however, Rika instantly commandeered this unwashed cowboy from Donnelly Dome to cut her winter's wood. Butch was glad to swap work for meals, and moved into a cabin upstream.

From the beginning, Rika shot her own rabbits. The local prospectors and trappers began to depend on the rabbit stew she kept ready on the stove.

For Sheldon's taxi passengers, she cooked moose stew, provided by Butch or any of the other bachelors who based around the roadhouse: Louis Grimsmore, the Johnson brothers, Steve Lowing, Teddy Goring or Carl Armstrom.

The Sale of the Roadhouse; McCarty's/Rika's

After Rika had worked a year for John, she still had not been paid. On the other hand, John did not want to run a roadhouse. Moreover, his wife had refused to come to Alaska to help him. Signing the roadhouse over to Rika seemed like a good solution. In 1918, the roadhouse became Rika's.

She finally had what she wanted, and she meant to hold onto it. Rika had watched her father lose Sodra Walla; she had suffered the disintegration of her family. The pain had seared a frugality deep into her that held her with a steel grip. As a result, Rika not only pioneered but kept the first homestead in Big Delta.

In 1920, Rika began a two year trip Outside (to the lower 48). While she was in Oakland, she organized her final move from California to a lifetime of running the McCarty roadhouse.

In the July 13, 1922 *Fairbanks Daily News-Miner,* it was reported that Rika and a "Miss Alice Riggs" had just returned from two years in the "States." It was said they were returning to the roadhouse "to resume their work."

State of Alaska Senator John Butrovich, a lifelong Fairbanks resident, recalled, "When I was growing up in Alaska in the 1920s, everyone knew that Rika and her sister ran the Big Delta roadhouse. They were called, 'the two old maids of Delta.' Oh, yeah, everyone knew that." Senator Butrovich's word was esteemed as "above reproach." It may possibly be that Maria Charlotta, Rika's sister, returned with Rika in 1922, not "Miss Alice Riggs," and worked with Rika throughout the 1920s.

Tuberculosis at Healy Lake and in the Upper Tanana, c. 1920

In 1975, Kathleen Newton Shafer, the daughter of the early trader, William Newton, wrote to her friend, Margaret Jacob Kirsteatter, "I can still recall when some of the Indians came to the trading post and first told Daddy or Mother that they were 'spitting up blood.' Almost all had tuberculosis. It is dreadful how the whites spread it to them and did almost nothing about it."

Kathleen continued, "When Chief Healy's daughter, Hootna's (Mary's) children were dying of TB and Meningitis, Mother, despite her own children, took food and nursed her friends."

The Newton children, Madge, Hal and Kathleen, were not allowed in the cabins during epidemics, Kathleen explained, but they could go in the tents.

Trying to escape the disease, Chief Sam moved his family to Sam Creek, southeast of the Healy River on the Tanana Crossing Trail.

As the sickness spread, Natives around Big Delta also became feverish. Rika began bringing food to their hide houses.

One day, a boy from the Goodpaster village appeared at her door. Epidemic had taken both of Abraham Luke's parents. He had walked 225 miles to McCarty needing a job. Rika gave him a bed under the stairs and some hot stew. Over the years, Abraham became an adopted son to John and Rika. First, he did odd jobs for Rika, then later, piloted trading boats for John.

Tetlin, Alaska, c. 1933

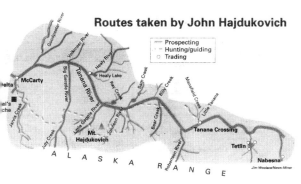

Prospecting
Hunting/guiding
Trading

John Hajdukovich's hunting camps: Beal's Cache-Little Gerstle River. Trading route: Healy River, Sam and Billy Creeks, Tanana-Crossing, Tetlin and Nabesna.

Trading

Growing up in Montenegro, John had frequently packed supplies along a river trail to his home, carrying the supplies either on his back or by horseback. It was natural, therefore, after the First World War shut mining down, for John to turn to hauling goods up the Tanana River to the isolated Natives.

Vuka Stepovich, an Alaskan who was also Montenegrin, said, "John was the nicest man who ever crossed the Atlantic."

She explained, "In that time, Native families lived in wall tents throughout the winter, trapping furs in remote river valleys. Whenever they needed anything, they sent word to John. He harnessed his dogs and brought them whatever they needed. 'Praise the Lord, John' is what the Natives called him," Vuka added with complete certainty.

Alice Jacob Joe of Healy Lake said, "John was the life support system for the Native people of the Upper Tanana. His stores at Healy River, his caches at Sam Creek and Billy Creek, as well as his stores at Tanana Crossing and Nabesna made life possible. He stocked a string of caches and allowed us to simply sign out goods as needed."

Her son, David Joe clarified, "Later, when the stores were called 'Native stores,' they were really John's."

"When did you establish your trading posts?" John was once asked.

He replied, "In 1918, I sold the roadhouse… I made a trip in 1919-20. I started in a small way, just got started. I got the trading post in both

Chief John Healy on John Hajdukovich's trading boat at McCarty's, c. 1917

places and hauled lots of stuff, lots of freight. I hauled quite a few tons over the Goodpaster trail.

He added, "I hada three trading posts: Tanana Crossing, they call it Tanacross; Tetlin; Nabesna, that's Northway now.

"We took supplies up the Tanana. Pretty rough going: Tanana River. We had gas boats. I had two gas boats. Could haul 4 or 5 tons each. Took five, six, seven, sometimes eight days from Big Delta to Tanacross."

On the way, John stocked a small store at Healy River and a series of caches all the way to the Canadian border, a distance of up to eleven days.

His expenses were high. He bought the best rifles, traps, and clothes, planned logistics carefully, and employed the most competent Natives.

As soon as the river was navigable in the spring, John launched his boat and began stocking for the new season. He and several Native deckhands pushed out from McCarty's. They hauled cable, axes, and food upriver, and often returned with passengers.

As they headed upstream, the wind was warm and the birds were flying. It was 135 river miles to Tanana Crossing. As they approached the few cabins, John's friend, Jack Singleton, came to greet them. They unloaded the *White Elephant*, John's gas powered launch.

The next day, they launched into the narrowing river, cutting deep into muskrat country.

John then turned into the mouth of the "Tetling" River. A plethora of waterfowl erupted as the boat swept around the curves of the narrow river. Mother birds faked a broken wing trying to distract the boat pilot from her chicks swimming as fast as their robotic feet could paddle.

The river thinned into a narrow ribbon as it neared Tetlin village. After they had unloaded the goods for the store, and hauled them to John's store, John checked

 on his hybrid wolf team. Some of his Native friends had wintered them at his Tetlin headquarters.

John Healy, Chief Walter Isaac, Paddy Healy, Peter Charles, Jimmy Walters, Pete Charlie, Andrew Isaac, Mansfield, c.1930

Tabessa, a little girl, liked to play close to John's wolves. They ran wildly on a slider the length of a cable line. John warned her playfully, "Getta too close, Tabessa … lose an arm!"

All summer, John and his Native pilots pushed hard getting loads up the river, but sometimes the

Double-ender sled, in overflow, crossing the Delta River, c. 1912

low water caught them. The supplies then had to be cached until they could return after freeze-up. The boat was dry-docked wherever the low water caught them, and John returned to McCarty's on foot.

When snow covered the muskeg, John hitched a horse to a double-ender sled to ferry his cached supplies to the Healy and Tetlin Rivers. For big loads, John used the horses. During the dead of winter, and for smaller loads, he relied on dogs. Whether he freighted by horse or by dog teams, several Natives worked for him.

The Clearwater/Healy/Tanana Crossing trail was, however, unduly narrow. For years, John had solicited the Alaska Road Commission to widen it. Two hundred Natives and prospectors of the Upper Tanana depended on it.

Still using the same rough trail, he crossed the Tanana to the Healy side. He watched for overflow, the pressurized ooze of water over river ice. Occasionally, overflow, or a horse plunging through rotten ice, might dampen flour and matches. Always, John had to wrap those goods in waxed muslin.

As he continued overland, he fought drifts and a narrow trail, working for every penny. If the load bogged, he hooked the horse to the other end of the "double-ender," and jerked the load loose. At twists in the trail, he made a wide berth to prevent the loaded sled from ramming into a tree.

Resembling an Arabian caravan, his parade through the Bush was a welcome sight in any of the villages.

Mary Gene, an elder in Tetlin, remembered, "When John came round the bend, everyone was happy!"

At Tetlin, he operated his store until spring's longer days. Then he hopped on his runners and pushed on to Nabesna. The snow sparkled in the brilliant sunshine. "Whoosh,"…his eager team vanished across the crust to the village nearest the Canadian border.

As John's team slowed, he saw the melted-in, crystallized prints of lynx and marten tracks and knew the season would soon be over.

Arriving in Nabesna, he pushed open the door to his store. Behind him, villagers filed, ready to sell. John waved to them, "Come on in!" As they handed him pelts, he calculated goods in exchange. If they could not pay, John simply skewered another I.O.U. note on the counter's spindle. By 1930, John's habit of never denying a customer was drowning him. Hoping that if someone else were handling the business profits might increase, John sold the business to Ted Lowell.

Ted later said he spent the winter up the river to protect John from his tendency "to give it all away." But even with John "safely" in Big Delta, if a Native needed something, John sent notes to Ted to "be sure and give" a needed item to the customer. The tall spindle of I.O.U.s on the counter became a pyramid by spring. Not able to pay John for the stores, and ready to return downriver, Ted turned the business back over to John.

John's supplies were purchased on credit from Northern Commercial Company, and from Bob Bloom, the Fairbanks outfitter. John's books, according to Ted Lowell, showed a debt of thirty thousand dollars, merchandise entrusted to his friends.

The official explanation of the sale of the business to Lowell was that business was not good. The stock market had crashed and fur prices were depressed. John was overloaded and it seemed like a good time to unload his trading business. John sold to Ted with the understanding that Lowell would buy him out completely in two years. When Lowell was not able to do so by 1931, John resumed his trading business.

The muskrat harvest was poor as well. John contended the season began too late, allowing the smaller ponds to routinely freeze to the bottom, killing the rats. No one profited. Muskrats brought the Natives fifty to seventy-five cents a piece. As the U.S. Game Commissioner, John pushed for the muskrat season to open earlier.

When spring returned to Nabesna every year, the muskrat hunters emerged in full force. The motto was, "Make hay while the sun shines." Families installed camps in the swamps and began killing, skinning, and eating "rats" twenty-four hours a day. The fur of the rats would not remain prime in the heat, so families worked furiously around the clock.

As quickly as the rats were shot, a family member gathered the carcasses in a wheelbarrow and hustled them to a skinner. It was the Natives' assembly line.

Swamping the Trail in 1919

Freighting on the Delta Cutoff with double-ender, c. 1912

The Clearwater/Healy/Tanana Crossing trail badly needed widening to accommodate the parade of double-ender sleighs pulled by nine horses, albeit single file. The trail was also a maze across unmarked river sloughs and through swamps.

John's petitions to the Board of Road Commissioners finally brought results. He was finally contracted to widen and stake 113 miles, bridge streams, and grade a corridor.

John's crew of Natives cleared trail from the Clearwater to Healy and George Lakes. They attempted to reach Sam Creek, but by then the budget was exhausted.

The improvement was noted in the *Fairbanks Daily News-Miner*, "John's new road to Tanana Crossing from McCarty, cut with the assistance of the A.R.C., is of great benefit and reduces time. Wide enough for horses and double-enders. It reduces transportation costs."

John, U.S. Commissioner, "the law from Fairbanks to the Canadian border"

When a Nabesna man shot a Canadian Athabaskan at Last Tetling, the U.S. Commissioner could not get free to investigate. In 1924, in an unusual move, Judge Cecil H. Clegg created John Hajdukovich U.S. Commissioner without power to preside at the inquest and hearing of the murderer.

As a result, John became "the law" from Big Delta to the border until 1936, when he quit in protest.

As commissioner during the 1930s, he appointed workers under the Roosevelt administration's Works Progress Administration program for the Civilian Conservation Corps to finally improve the trails of the Upper Tanana.

Milo Began Trading "Inside" the Agreement in 1922

John was over-loaded; he had a lot of irons in the fire. By 1920, he was noted in the *Fairbanks Daily News-Miner* as "the well known roadhouse man and freighter." Additionally he was in process of becoming a big game guide. Much had to be done. Horses had to be imported, wall tent platforms, and cabins built for wealthy clientele.

If that were not enough, John was also the U.S. Commissioner responsible for all legal proceedings from Big Delta to the border.

Feeling overwhelmed, John, in 1922, asked Milo to join him trading on the Upper Tanana. "John's name was a real help to Milo," Carl Tweiten recalled, "and Milo knew how to use it."

John had important stipulations, however. Milo was not to own his own store, gas boat, or do business for longer than two years.

Milo, whose mind was strictly that of a businessman's, soon had not only three stores, but a gas boat as well. Several times, when John told Milo the two years were up, Milo retorted that too many people still owed him money. He felt it was necessary to keep going until everything due him was re-paid.

Milo was competing with his cousin, John, Herman Kessler at Nabesna, Ole Fredrickson at Tanana Crossing, Emil Hammer at Healy and C.D. Flannigan at Tetlin.

Herman Kessler with mail carrier, spring trail c. 1919

"John was easy prey for everyone in Big Delta," Carl Tweiten said. "John kept his supplies in the old Bennett trading post. Everyone dipped into the warehouse: everyone. John was easy to take advantage of. It just didn't matter enough to him to pay close attention."

Continuing to work more or less together, "the Hajdukovich brothers," as the *Fairbanks Daily News-Miner* called them in June 1925, "brought in two large truckloads of furs."

John and Milo could finally mail furs directly from Big Delta. Rika was the postmistress and annually, they mailed sixty thousand dollars worth of furs from McCarty's. Before each sale was made, and before every shipment went out, John telegraphed the Seattle Fur Exchange to check current fur prices.

Caravan double-enders on glaciated overflow Alaska Range pass, c. 1912

The Bison Herd Importation

As one who harvested the land and also guarded it, John said, "The catches of fur, however, are not as rich as they once were. They are a fraction of what they once were." He added, "This may end in the wilderness, once peopled with living things, becoming nothing but a dream …"

It was a stark possibility, not withstanding the wilderness was "the bank" for both John and the Natives. He worried, too, that the Natives' food supply might seriously dwindle. He pushed for importing Montana bison to Delta, to undergird the situation. His concerns were complimented by a Fairbanks sportsmen's group led by Game Warden Frank Dufresne.

For years, Orr Stage Line's horses had fed well on the protein-rich, pea vines of the Delta river. John reasoned the

Ted Lowell's "Richardson Freight and Stage," on Shaw Creek Bluff, hauling twenty-three crated bison to Big Delta, 1928

59

Orr Stage Line's horses foraging at Donnelly Roadhouse, c. 1912

buffalo would do well with it also. In 1928, the sportsmen imported twenty-three bison, which arrived by train.

From the railroad, Ted Lowell's Richardson Freight and Stage trucks picked up the crated calves. Two crates, each containing a bison calf weighing 1200-1500 pounds apiece, were put onto each truck. At Big Delta, the trucks rode across the Tanana on the ferry. Teddy Goring set the rudder and carried them from the north to the south bank. A stockade had been prepped on the south side to allow the animals to rest a few days before their release.

John helped Ted unload the crates and free the animals into a pen just south of the roadhouse. Throughout the following winter, Louis Grimsmore, Rika's handyman, spot-checked the bison. Periodically, it was reported they were adapting well to the wind-swept Delta.

As to whether the bison ever supplanted the Natives' diet, Josephine Beaver said, "Natives never liked bison! They called them 'white man's cattle!'"

The Interior's Most Recognized Big Game Guide

Hajduk's Outfitter: Bob Bloom

About 1903, a Russian Jewish immigrant in Dawson saw his opportunity. The profits to be made were not in striking gold, but in supplying those seeking the gold. The Waechter brothers had already begun herding cattle into the large gold camps and were hiring wranglers. Bob Bloom signed up and became a Russian cowboy, walking the beef all the way from Canada to Alaska's Chena River.

From the profits of his salary, Bloom starting loaning money to the prospectors: "grubstaking" them. When they could not repay their loan, Bloom would "inherit" their assets. With the claims he collected, he invested further in a store on Second Avenue in Fairbanks, naming it: "R. Bloom." It quickly became the outfitting headquarters for the Bush.

Bloom was also a main supplier to John Hajdukovich. Not only were Bloom and John both Slavic, but as Bloom once told his daughter, "John and I understand each other. We are both traders."

"John," Bloom's daughter, Meta Bloom, added, "maintained a mailing address at Dad's store. He was often in our home and was always a handsome and respected guest, the consummate gentleman, a cut above everyone else."

Her father's store, on Front Street, between Cushman and Lacey, she said, was a gathering place for debate, a sort of "intellectual's delicatessen."

Back East, Bloom had extensive

John Hajdukovich, big game guide, packing Wendell Endicott's trophy caribou, 1927

61

John, hunter's trophy grizzly, 'Granites,' Alaska Range, 1927

contacts with wealthy sportsmen interested in Alaskan big game hunting, known as "The Campfire Club." They asked Bloom to find them a quality hunt. Bloom knew John Hajdukovich had the class, the endurance, and the eye to do a first class safari. Bloom backed Hajdukovich in buying twenty-four horses and put him in touch with wealthy industrialists. By February 1924, John was driving eight head of horses at –68° F. into Tanana Crossing, to begin the business.

Beal's Cache, a roadhouse near Donnelly Dome, was the jumping-off point for John's hunts. Located in good hunting country at an elevation of 1600 feet, Beal's was a single story, unpeeled log building on the east side of the road. Like the stage horses and the bison, John's twenty-four horses foraged on the protein-rich vetch of the Delta River.

Both "Butch" Stock and "Jack" Ray took care of John's horses at Beal's and at the Little Gerstle River.

When John had off time, he mapped out blue ribbon hunts for his millionaire clients. He even included oranges and eggs for breakfast before they went out to stalk sheep, caribou, moose, and grizzly in the hills.

In His Glory

The *Fairbanks Daily News-Miner* throughout the 1920s and early '30s described John as "bringing much wealth to Alaska."

In 1924, John was heralded as "the recognized guide of the Interior." The *News-Miner* added, "Each year, John gets more and more hunters."

William N. Beach, one of John's most repeat clients said, "If we told John we want to go next morning and go the next day and the day after and the day after that, John would say, 'All right! And ready to go!'"

"Just because John can go and likes to go, he will probably live longer and go on forever. He is one loveable vagabond."

Beach, who had once tracked a 32 inch Dall ram for three days with John, wrote John from Africa. "I wouldn't trade one foot of Alaska for all of Africa," he said.

Another client, Harold Keith, in his book, *A Hunting Trip In the Interior Of Alaska, During the Summer of 1930,* said, "John was always the quiet, cheerful leader, the cool and clear thinker. He inspired us with his confidence."

Wendell Endicott of Boston, in the fall of 1927, rode with John deep into the Alaska Range. In his book, Endicott described John's competent guiding.

He noted John always cached provisions far afield, in case his hunters might overextend during their stalk.

Even though John was fifty-two by this time, he easily sped ahead of his hunters. Like a mountain goat on Mount Hajdukovich's ramparts, he scaled the slope ahead of them to spot sheep and caribou for his men.

In 1927, his focus set, his bearing relaxed, John led Wendell Endicott over the high plateau looking for a silver tipped, huge bear. From time to time, they spotted the bear whenever he stood, and then they lost him again as he fed. John's senses were completely connected to that bear. He would not give up. As they waited, Endicott's tied up horse scented the bear and began to get excited.

Much later, Endicott asked John, "What would you have done if the horse had spooked during the kill?" John replied in his laconic manner …, "Just turn him loose and deal with him later."

After a successful all-day stalk, John simply turned to his client and suggested, "Let's get a bite of lunch."

For the ensuing weeks, they followed sheep, caribou, and moose, often in the snow. John worked with his Native wranglers, always packing the game and handling the horses.

Robert Bloom and John in the pink roadhouse with Rika's chicken wire partition, c.1960

Endicott observed John as he dealt with both Natives and the hunters, "John always has a kindly thought … giving tokens of his never-ceasing good-will.

"It was interesting and instructive to see the way he talks to and treats the Native. He understands them better than any man I ever met."

After two months, the grizzled hunters, wranglers, and heavily-laden horses gingerly descended to the snow-dusted wall tents near Morning Star creek. At Little Gerstle river camp, Chief John Healy led the horses to the wild grass pastures. The next day, the triumphant hunters rode in John's canvas-protected boat to their waiting wives at Rika's Roadhouse.

Endicott and his hunting partner had both filled their hunting limits. Later he wrote in his journal what they had shot: "3 sheep, 3 caribou, 2 grizzly, 3 black bear, 1 moose, and 1 bountied wolf." (For just Endicott.) "In over twenty days", he noted, "they saw 23 grizzly, 16 black bear, 741 sheep, 1019 caribou, 25 moose, 2 fox, 12 wolves, and 1 coyote."

For "dessert" that night, John entertained the men and their wives with the story of Healy Lake and "the famous potlatch of 1927."

The Potlatch of 1927

Born in 1868, Chief Healy was fifty-nine when his children, Paddy, Mary and John, honored him with a potlatch celebrated in the grand old style. The motive of the potlatch was a profound display of honor in giving to others all that one possessed. People saved for years, gathering blankets, rifles, and teapots, to lavish on "most precious guests."

The July 1927 *Fairbanks Daily News-Miner* reported, "It was a

Paddy, Mary (Hoatna) and John Healy, 1927 potlatch honoring Old Chief Healy

celebration at Healy Lake like….before the invasion of the white men.

"Five hundred blankets rippled in the breeze off the old village hill, and fifty guns saluted the incoming guests arriving from as far as the Copper River."

Special cabins, with imported planed floors, had been built for the party. Kathleen Newton Shafer remembered, "People traveled the trails from the Crossing, Nabesna, and Tetlin for the potlatch. When the men of Balzulnetas ['Bah-zoolnetuhz] arrived, they were greeted with rifle fire at the Healy River's mouth." The rifle fire was not aimless, according to Endicott. From an angle, it was pointed at a certain spot, making a trajectory, as if a sweeping arm were ushering its guests in an embrace.

3rd rt: Harold Newton, Joe Joseph, & Andrew Isaac playing mouth organ, 1927 potlatch, Healy Lake

Kathleen continued, "When the guests climbed the village hill to honor the chief, racks of Hudson Bay blankets greeted them.

"Countless provisions were purchased and transported to that little village, sitting so peacefully on the bluff above the lake," Endicott described.

Kathleen, her family, and their guest, Patricia Hering, as well as John Hajdukovich, were the only white guests attending. Kathleen said, "Many of the goods had been purchased from our store for just that occasion."

The *Fairbanks Daily News-Miner,* July 25, 1927, continued: "From Copper River, from Tetling, from Tanana Crossing and all the sweeping territory between, Indians made their way to Healy River to observe once more their tribal rites.

"Healy River consists of only seven or eight cabins and of several families. The village gave away five hundred blankets, fifty guns, and spread a feast each night for five days. Seventy-five natives visited.

"Daytimes were devoted to resting and preparing for the coming activities of the evening. Healy River men alternated in making the banquets ready.

"When the sun began to dip toward the horizon, the Indians gathered in a circle and commemorated the dead in mourning songs.

"When the homage had been paid to the dead, they seated themselves on the floor of the big meeting cabin, ready for the feast. Beginning with servings of moosehead soup, followed by hardtack, dried meat, doughnuts and canned fruit.

The banquet proceeded slowly and was accompanied by rituals less modern than the food.

"With their hunger satisfied, the potlatchers once more bethought themselves of their ancestors and again mourned for them in song.

"Then began the impressive Indian dances, which lasted for hours. The tribal dance of the southern Indians from Copper River differed from those of the others. A booming tom-tom from a moosehide drum beat steadily through the half-dusk. The four chiefs present sat together, looking on approvingly.

Agnes Jacob and Old Chief Healy, Healy Lake, c. 1919

"The dancers slowed, stopped. A young man stepped to one side, wound a machine and in another instant jazz strains of the latest dance record superseded the drum. And so, far into the morning, the feet which had only a short while ago moved to the commanding boom of the drum, took their cue from the music of New York and San Francisco dance orchestras.

"Each day this program was repeated. At times from the banquet floor, men would rise to make speeches. The Copper River Indians talked slowly, so their friends might understand the slightly different dialect."

They spoke of who was related to whom, of intermarriages, oral records of blood relationships. Since there were no written documents, it was a safeguard against intermarriage. "How else," Josephine Beaver asked, "could Natives from Copper River to Big Delta know who was a relative…?"

The *News-Miner* continued, "Some of the visitors received as much as 12 blankets and two guns. When a man did not like the pattern of the blanket or kind of gun presented to him, he would at once make known his desires and ask for the objects of his choice. All the gifts were presented on the last afternoon of the potlatch. Tanana Crossing, Tetling and Copper River Indians at once began selling and trading their gifts with full approval of their hosts.

"After they had given the blankets and guns, Healy River natives insisted upon giving the visitors parkas, and almost all the food in the village. They even tried to press their cooking utensils upon the departing guests."

"Chief Joe canoed from George Lake for the celebration," remembered Jeanie Healy. "When the potlatch was over, he just shouldered his canoe and walked home." Even automobiles were provided to return the Copper River Natives to their homes, a five hundred mile round trip for their hosts. Much of these expenses were funded by a loan from John Hajdukovich to the chief.

Endicott wrote, "After it was all over and the guests were departing, old Chief Healy drew John aside. There was a deep and radiant smile of satisfaction upon the old chief's lips, almost to the point of tears. 'John, they have it all,' he said. 'You have helped me lots…They have it all. If I die tonight, I die happy.'"

Many times after a potlatch not even a crumb of bread was left in the village.

In the spring of 1928, before Chief Healy died, the chief boated a cache load of furs to John to repay him.

John counseled a friend afterward, "Don't ever underestimate a man. There is always a better man than you are."

John was, however, bothered by the destitution resulting from the lavish potlatches. The entire cost in 1927, paid for by only eight families, was … twenty thousand dollars. Speaking to Endicott, John said, "This terrific extravagance and self deprivation is most unfortunate. I am doing my best; urging them to stop it. They really need their savings against bad years and old age. I hope these affairs will cease."

John did obtain an old age pension for the Natives, but for himself, he made no provision. To such things, John characteristically replied in his laconic way, "Oh, I never bothered with any of that."

The potlatch occurred in the days before alcohol, epidemics, and the divisive wedge of big money and politics.

Healy Lake village 1930s.

The Roadhouse

Citizenship

I n 1922, John Hajdukovich attained his citizenship, as did Robert Bloom and William Newton. John described himself on his application: "5 feet 10 inches, brown hair, brown eyes, married." Before his forty-fourth birthday, John became an American.

Patenting the Roadhouse, Redeeming "Her Once Lost Estate"

In the spring, lawyers and bankers enjoyed Sunday drives to Delta for dining at Rika's. During those visits, Rika's professional friends advised her to file for a homestead patent. Rika "staked for a patent right over the top of the roadhouse, up and down the river, and across the highway: 320 acres," according to Ted Lowell.

Rika officially changed her name, as well, from Lovisa Erika Jakobsson to "Rika Wallen," coined from Sodra Wallen, her farm in native Sweden.

Building a Roadhouse

Rika had changed her name, and similarly, she wanted to change the casual handle of "McCarty," applied to the roadhouse. Reacting to the 1919 murder of

Rika purchasing goat, Oakland, California, c. 1920

young Dan McCarty, she exclaimed indignantly to her hired girl, Florence Holmes in 1938, "It yust ain't no good! My roadhouse won't be called by the name of no murderer!"

"McCarty" was also too similar to the name of another Alaskan community, "McCarthy." The confusion had once resulted in the Army Signal Corp's winter rations being accidentally delivered to McCarthy on the Copper River. The Big Delta military reservation's name was subsequently changed to "Grundler."

Rika's Roadhouse: Seated L-R: Louis Grimsmore, builder/handyman; Teddy Goring, ferry operator; possibly Mary Hellsten, Rika's sister; Ted Lowell, freighter; Henry "Butch" Stock Standing L-R: Charlie Lockhart & Rika Wallen

For both the Signal Corps and for Rika's buildings, boards were needed for expansion. Lumber had to be whipsawed by hand. This was frequently done by two Natives, one on either end of the saw pushing and pulling, making one board at a time.

John's Native friends from up and down the river earned one dollar an hour working for Rika, as well as receiving room and board. Silas Solomon of Ketchumstuk, the Healy brothers, and Abraham Luke all worked for Rika to bring in the 17 tons of hay required for her cows, geese and sheep. As a result, she was the first person in the Interior to produce wool. She also had a greenhouse, a small orchard and the first aviary.

Where Milo Hajdukovich had once raised fox, Louis Grimsmore built cages for Rika's six new pairs of silver fox.

In a 1923 photo, traces of the improvements were seen in the fresh lumber stacked next to the roadhouse. Grimsmore, the ferryman and handyman, had asked John to buy a number twelve, portable sawmill and planer. This meant it was no longer necessary to cross-cut logs into lumber in the slow, primitive manner, but instead lumber was made by using an efficient steam driven assembly. With it, Grimsmore built the 1927 addition to the roadhouse.

Rika the Farmer

"Rika worked like a man," Silas Solomon said. "She was a farmer first, and a cook second. She did, however, serve delicious chicken dinners and bear fat pastry pie."

"Rika kept bees, goats, cows, and chickens," Carl Tweiten bragged. "For her cattle, I built her a windmill." Fresh milk, from her registered Holsteins, was a rare treat in the wilderness. She maintained her herd with culled calves from Creamer's Dairy in Fairbanks. She kept all her perishables cool in the spring house.

Kathy Zachgo, a homesteader, said, "When Rika had to milk, she went looking for the cows. She always hoped the buffalo were not visiting."

"Once," Kathy grinned, "the bison kept Rika holed up in the barn for hours."

"It was a real menagerie at the roadhouse," Kathy smiled. "Everyone ran loose: the cows, the chickens, and John's horses. Their hooves sounded like thunder beating the ground: twenty-four of them on a dead run."

Even the aviary got loose. "Rika wintered her bees," remembered Alaska Linck of Fairbanks, "in her root cellar."

Alaska continued, "Once, when we were dining in the roadhouse, the bees woke up! Suddenly, the whole roadhouse was filled with bees! We ran for cover!"

In the spring, Rika gathered dandelions for her specialty: dandelion wine. By the 1940's, she had a "one lung" generator, which did little more than supply enough power for the lights, but every day, she needed someone to start it. Those who jump-started it also got a jolt of a large tumbler of her dandelion wine.

Local bachelors traded work for meals, but sometimes their credit outweighed their labor. Carl Tweiten, however, worked around the clock.

"We harvested wild grass all the way to Four Mile Hill using John Hajdukovich's horses," Carl remembered. "I used John's mower. My brother,

Rika, Lila Mae, Walter and Bob Johnson, c.1930

Oscar, gathered Billy Mitchell's old telegraph wire. We stretched it between posts, making wire racks every 18 inches, just clearing the tops of the poles.

"In Norway, we called that, 'hesha:' our way of preserving prime grass. We dried the wild grass in the Tanana wind."

"Rika as a farmer," Carl added, "was years ahead of her time."

"John planted potatoes," Carl continued, "on a small hillside on the other side of the Delta riverbank near the old roadhouse. He also planted a potato patch on Hanson Hollow's bluff.

"Maybe they had the same idea in Montenegro as in Norway— that potatoes should be grown on a sunny, warm hillside," mused Carl.

While Big Delta had the same midnight sun, flowers, and similar winters as Sweden, it was as raw as Stockholm was elegant. Rika remembered the dignity of Europe and looked around for materials; she spotted the wooden kerosene crates. Kerosene was packaged in five gallon cans, two to a wooden box. She pried the wooden sides loose and laid them at angles to each other on the floor, designing her own Alaskan "parquet" floor.

After the harvest was in, and the tourists were gone, Rika caned her chairs and knit sweaters from her sheep's wool. John always wore a hand-knit sweater-vest; always, he wore it, no matter its condition.

The New Wing of the Roadhouse, Transport and Communications

In 1926, Rika asked her Swedish handyman, Louis Grimsmore, to double her hostelry. With the added wing, the roadhouse became one of the trail's largest, able to house sixty. Grimsmore also built a cabin for Teddy Goring, the ferryman.

By the late 1920s, tourists no longer had to yell to get a ride across the Tanana, as they had before 1909. Motorists simply rang a bell and Goring sailed across the Tanana with the new 1926 ferry, charging truckers one dollar, and others, a dollar fifty.

But there was no telegraph. For five years, the telegraph station had been closed. Emergency communication would continue through a fifty watt, ham radio station installed in 1926, by the U.S. War Department.

Even though it was limited, the Alaska Road Commission installed telephone lines in 1929. The new system from Fairbanks (140 miles north) to Black Rapids, however, differed in signal from the telephone servicing from Black Rapids to the south. When critical, the Black Rapids roadhouse owner listened to the Fairbanks line with one ear, and repeated the message into the receiver pressed to her other ear: becoming "a human repeater."

Bob Redding, an Alaskan pioneer, said, "Rika, like everyone else, was on a party line, but hers stretched from Big Delta to Fairbanks. All homes had a particular ring, a unique signal."

Laughing, Bob continued, "If Rika were out hanging laundry when her ring came, she might just say, 'Ah, the hell with it…' and not bother to answer it."

"But," Florence Holmes recalled, "if she thought it might be the weather bureau, she answered it. Many Fairbanksans checked to see if the ferocious Delta winds were blowing before making a trip to Delta. To that question, Rika always responded quickly, 'No vend today.'"

The Happy Days of Trading

John reviewed trading at its best: before liquor, and before big government, when he was a witness at a 1963 State of Alaska trial. The lawyer asked, "How did you take your freight up?" John answered, "I had a horses. I took mine on a gas boats. But, I used to have twenty-four head of horses, but I didn't use them all on that trail. I used seven, eight to ten. Made quite a few trips during the winter, and that's the expensive. Take the rest of the time to cover? (that distance) five, six, seven, eight, and nine (days)"

Lawyer: "What was the traffic along the trail during those years? How many trips did you make during the winter?"

John: "Uh, overland. I used to make quite a few times. I used to get twelve to fifteen Indians, with a dog teams to Big Delta, and sometimes clear from Salchaket, to haul the freight with the dogs. Some of the other traders had to have the dogs, but some of them tried to haul up the river."

Lawyer: "Right, were there any traders up there?"

John: "One at Healy River, one at Healy Lake, and there was three traders on the upper Tanana. Or more… Let's see. What year did you say? 1924?

The Debutantes of Fairbanks and the Tetlin Potlatch

In 1931, after John and Milo had stocked most of their stores for the season, they invited Helen Franklin Heath, Helen MacDonald Straiger, Mrs. Julian Hurley, and Alaska Stewart (Linck) for an outing to Tanana Crossing. Probably...John was encouraging Milo to marry. Perhaps, Milo was "shopping."

The girls packed a Victrola to the potlatch held in their honor. They demonstrated the most recent dance steps. To her great amusement, Martha Isaac of Tanacross, remembered the display to this day.

In return, the Natives chanted the ancient songs of the potlatch. They fed them the traditional moose head soup and presented each girl with a new Hudson's Bay blanket. Alaska remembered that on the way home the over-loaded boat narrowly missed hitting the Johnson River bluffs.

Helen Franklin Heath, John, Helen MacDonald Straiger, Mrs. Julian Hurley, Alaska Stewart Linck, 1931, Tanana Crossing

"Well, there was Flannigan, Herman Kessler, myself, Milo Hajdukovich is my cousin, Lawrence De Witt and Oly Aspen, they used to trade."

Lawyer: "Anybody at Healy River?"

John: (with respectful indifference:) "Newton." (With a lilt:) "Newton." (Finally, in a set tone:) "Newton" (with pensive thoughts), "Yeah."

Lawyer: "Where did this fellow Hammer go that you spoke about?

John: "Hammer bought Newton's trading post."

Lawyer: "Newton was there in 1904?

John: "Ah, yes he was. And, De Witt had a cabin at Last Tetlin, but he had a trading post at Mentasta. At first, he was only trader at Last Tetlin, but after that, he was just buying fur. Seven mile difference between Tetlin and Last Tetlin.

"Yeah, but I bought this cabin at Tetlin and I used to buy fur from Lawrence. Yeah, we served the same people. I didn't trade at Mentasta, but he traded. Maybe five, six, seven, eight families at Mentasta. Course some of them was Lawrence's family.

"Kessler traded at Nabesna village, but he had his store up at Chisana, close to Scottie Creek. Then, he built a cabin close to Nabesna village, that's a Northway now. Kessler traded with fifteen to twenty, maybe thirty people up there. But, Indians trade every place. They don't want a trading post even if they have to go 30 miles to another trading post. They will trade anyplace."

The freighter for the traders was Ted Lowell. He reported his trucks, Richardson Trail: Freight and Stage, hauled 200 tons annually for the traders.

After picking up the goods, the traders freighted upriver using their 195 horsepower motors. Emil Hammer ferried to Healy River; Flannigan to Tetlin; Kessler to Nabesna; and the Hajdukoviches to all three villages.

In 1927, the aviation age came to the Bush when A.A. Bennett flew a plane to Tetlin Lake.

Peter, Lucy and Kenny Thomas

Kenny Thomas of Tanacross said, "My parents, Peter and Lucy Thomas, were very well thought of. They were nice,… real nice people.

He added, "My wife, Ellen Thomas' father, Joe Joseph, was born very early in Big Delta, in 1886. He lived into the 1960s. But my parents… got sick when I

A Christmas Story By Chief Walter Northway's Daughter, Enna Albert of Nabesna/Northway

When John traded up the Tanana, Christmas was a time of renewing friendship, giving fresh slippers, and having food to share.

Enna, Chief Northway's daughter, was aware December 25th was some sort of holiday. In 1937, she had seen a Santa Claus. But it was not until the construction of the Alcan highway in 1942, though, that she really knew the word, "Christmas."

In Tetlin, however, trader Herman Kessler had taught Helen David about the birth of Christ. The Davids, who lived closer to St. Timothy's mission at Tanana Crossing, had heard of Christmas traditions since 1910-15. Enna, however, had been on a trapline up the Ladue River, close to the Canadian border, and had been isolated from outside influences, so she knew very little about Christmas.

One day, she leaned back and began to tell the story of when, as she grew, she began to experience the holiday. After Christmas was introduced in Northway, Native festivities were integrated into the holy day. To celebrate, the village extracted, from the muskrat caches, a sweet tubular grass called "muskrat candy."

74

was only twelve. They got sick on the trapline: one of the epidemics. First, my sister and then, my parents—; they lay dead in the tent... and I crawled out... they... were all dead.

"I had to get a job. I had a little brother and sister to take care of. I went to John Hajdukovich and asked him, 'could I get a job?'

"Carefully, he looked at me... and was quiet, 'You think you can handle it?' he asked. 'Yes,' I said and he said, 'Okay, start work tomorrow... as a deckhand.'"

"It was hard work; it wasn't any fun," Thomas remembered of his years with John. "At the Johnson River, we winched a load many times around the bluff. Two different river currents hit the rock's straight face at a 90° angle, causing bad whirlpools. We dumped a load more than once. In late fall, we battled low water and ice. We took lots of chances."

"Once, I said to him, 'OH, JOHN! Why don't you go back that country you come from?!' He simply sighed, and waved his hand...and said, 'Ah...that country...'"

Kenny continued, "John was good-hearted. He liked to help people. He always talked about reasonable things. He fought to keep alcohol out of the Upper

---

hey diced this cat tail, mixed it with stored greens, and fried both in moose fat. The esult was a celery flavor, further enhanced with cranberries and blueberries. Moose ead soup simmered on the wood "barrel" stove for the villagers. Rice and biscuits dded heft to the Christmas meal.

To prepare for Christmas Day, ladies had been sewing new slippers for weeks. As e day approached, the men gathered firewood. John Hajdukovich mushed in three ans of Christmas candy, while Herman Kessler freighted in loads of dried meat.

On Christmas Day, the custom was that villagers traveled from house to house ith a willow hook and long stick, pulling a sled behind. The people tapped on each oor. If amends were in order, hands were clasped in friendship. Also, when the illow hook was presented, the donor slipped money or meat onto the prong. Each ouseholder then changed into fresh clothes and joined the procession to the ommunity center where Christmas dinner waited. Following the courses of meats, erries and greens, dancers filled the floor and played games. Tetlin school teacher, ack Singleton, taught villagers the "two-step," while John Hajdukovich smiled armly, happy to be there, simply the observer that he was.

Enna's brother-in-law, Oscar Albert, said, "It was a happy time. People helped ach other."

Tanana. He said it defeated his reason for trading up the river. He, and all the traders, kept alcohol out until 1932. But finally, Herman Kessler wanted the easy profits and he began bringing it in."

McCarty/Rika's with John's trading boats, c. 1932

Robert McKennan's Athabaskan Base Study of the Upper Tanana

In 1930, pristine, aboriginal cultures were becoming difficult for anthropologists to find. Before the advent of liquor in the region, Dartmouth College professor, Dr. Robert A. McKennan, discovered the purity of the isolated Upper Tanana-Athabaskan culture. He flew to Alaska to study it in depth. John Hajdukovich, also a student of the Athabaskans, escorted him to the area.

The *Fairbanks Daily News-Miner* wrote: "McKennan selected the Upper Tanana 'because Indians there have had less contact with whites than at other places.' His studies established a base study for Athabascan, the family of all Mackenzie and Interior Alaskan Indians. McKennan traveled on a Harvard University fellowship. He entered the McCarty country, traveling through the White, Chisana and Nabesna river districts to the various Indian villages. He spent the winter collecting data, including Native social and religious customs. He talked with older men, but did not overlook anyone. He found Indians willing to aid to the best of their ability. All were able, more or less, to speak English, but it was necessary to carry on conversations with some of the oldest men through younger natives who had been educated. He credits success of his trip to the cooperation of the white people who went out of their way to make themselves helpful."

Dr. McKennan autographed a copy of his book, "To John Hajdukovich, a fellow student of these Indians whose friendly advice and helping hand along the trail contributed so much to my study of the Upper Tanana. 30 July 62, Bob McKennan."

The Tetlin Reserve

*John's Shift From Trading to the Reserve;
John, the Connective Tissue Between
the Natives and Their Needs*

Over campfires, John, Wendell Endicott, and Edward Mallinckrodt planned "the noblest of solutions," according to Tanacross Council President, Jerry Isaac. In 1930, their solution became known as "The Tetlin Reserve." John longed to see his Athabaskan friends protected as well as trained and equipped for assimilation into the modern world. He felt that a federal reserve, implemented by governmental resources and under governmental control was the answer. Around the campfire, John and his hunters envisioned a school, a clinic, and a post office, all sustained by a village economy.

They drew up plans and petitioned to have 625 square miles of public land at Tetlin withdrawn from public domain. The acreage would be a federal reserve managed by the Office of Indian Affairs. The Tetlin Reserve would be developed by the Natives with guidance from the federal government.

Edward Mallinckrodt of St. Louis, Wendell Endicott of Boston, and John Hajdukovich imagined a fur ranch, sustained with a farming crop in the village. They worked with Chief Peter Joe of Tetlin, who fully supported the ideas.

In 1930, Earl J. Beck, the Bureau of Education's Division Superintendent, mushed with John to Tetlin to consider the Natives' need for a school. Beck was forced by temperatures of -50° F. to spend two weeks with Chief Peter Joe's people at Tetlin. After such close living with the village and their fourteen school age children, Beck commended John for "jealously guarding the Natives to see that no harmful influence shall come upon them."

*Master big game guide,
John Hajdukovich, 1927*

77

Chief Peter Joe family, with Helen David between the adults, Tetlin, c. 1935

Tetlin was unusual in its pure condition, and Beck credited John as a courageous and honest man. Beck also added that both Milo and John did not gouge the Natives for fur profits. He felt the freighting conditions warranted the prices paid.

The following summer, Dr. Carlson Ryan Jr., the Director of Education in the Office of Indian Affairs, visited the Upper Tanana by boat. He was also very impressed seeing the work Jack Singleton and John had done with the people. The Native people, with John and Jack's help, had built their own school and bridge using lumber they had "ripped" themselves. The people were clean and healthy. (Natives elsewhere were infected with Tuberculosis and Whooping Cough, and even soap could be a rare commodity.) Further, Ryan observed that Singleton had taught the Natives how to use a tractor, and together, they had made a garden out of 4 acres.

Many options for Native transition to the modern age were under consideration. It was generally conceded that lower 48 reservations had been a patent failure. Alaska was attempting to educate the Native children within the village, not removing them to a boarding school. The proposal of a village industry, envisioned by John and his wealthy friends, caught Ryan's interest.

In 1930, for the first time in twenty-seven years, John traveled Outside to see his influential friends, Mallinckrodt and H. Wendell Endicott, to discuss the Tetlin Reserve. Endicott had written a letter to President Hoover, which was delivered to the President just as he was considering the reserve. Everything fell perfectly into place, and an executive order was signed June 10, 1930. Consequently, four hundred thousand acres was withdrawn from the public domain. Earnest Walker Sawyer, a special representative for the Alaska Railroad, announced that in five years, he expected Natives to be trained in fur farming. Further, Natives were encouraged to form more reserves.

Mallinckdrodt donated five thousand dollars for a tractor, sawmill, farming equipment, and seed potatoes. However, both the Office of Indian Affairs, and the Bureau of Education, claimed they were not authorized to oversee the operation.

Depressed fur prices and the onset of the Great Depression doomed the success of the Tetlin fur farm from its inception. Additionally, John was distracted when he had to repossess his trading business from Ted Lowell and resume trading. Worse, Dr. Ryan never really supported the Tetlin vision. He was pessimistic regarding the Natives' ability to carry off the utopian ideas. (His posture may have been fueled by E.A. McIntosh's opposition to the reserve.)

In further sabotage, Ryan refused to give John a salary to supervise the fur farm. The "industrial school," which was to be a fur farm, was dead before it began. The caterpillar and sawmill were sometimes rented for local construction, but the cottage industry never developed.

John had to turn from the interests of the Tetlin Reserve just to keep himself financially afloat. Jerry Isaac, today's Tanacross Council President, said "It was the grandest sort of plan. I wish my forefathers had done that for us."

Trading and the Office of Indian Affairs

"Grasping Straws"

Because John had lost heavily in mining, and since the Natives still owed him a large debt, John proposed a Native-owned store that he would initially oversee. One of the store's purposes was to pay back the debt owed him.

Liquor On the Upper Tanana - 1932

John claimed Kessler broke the traders' agreement in 1932 and began shipping in liquor. First, he shipped in 3 tons, and then, in 1938, he brought in 50 tons. The liquor came first to Nabesna, then from there, he traded to all the villages. When the cases of liquor began to arrive, Tetlin elder, Alfred John, said, "We just thought it was bottles of syrup, pancake syrup…"

The Native leaders were so alarmed that they publicly pleaded, "Please don't bring in any alcohol."

When John was sure all the traders were selling liquor, he tried boycotting, an old Serbian custom. He quit his post in protest, resigning as U.S. Commissioner in 1936. However, this resulting lack of authority only removed the fear of him, deleting "his stick." The door for liquor swung further open.

John had always adamantly opposed the easy profits of alcohol. Although Kessler had been "validated," by obtaining government and mission contracts, he was at the same time importing large amounts of booze. John asked Mallinckrodt to help.

Mallinckrodt wanted a second opinion, and paid an investigator, Moris Burge of the American Association on Indian Affairs Inc., to check into the situation.

The Evolving Crack Between Natives and Traders; Government and Native "Self-Determination"

Burge reconnoitered the Upper Tanana with John in 1938. He was sufficiently impressed with John. He said, "The Tetlin area in which John does his trading and offers his hospitality is somewhat a paradise under any conditions, with abundant game, fur, and fishing. With John Hajdukovich to help them over the rough spots, the Indians have found living very much worth the effort.

"In his business with the Indians, John has never let his personal interest stand in the way of decent humanity. He has made it his constant effort to keep sobriety and industry at the highest possible point among the Indian Alaskan patrons.

"Largely as a result of his insistent efforts, the Tetlin Indians have maintained a clean, straight thinking, and nobility of character that speaks well for the lives they live. Their genuine, wholesome way of living has given them a share of pride not often found among the more discouraged Alaskan Indians of other sections. John has helped keep the standards and has thereby brought real lasting wealth to the Territory.

"The Indians relied on him for matters of all importance, and had it not been for his influence, the picture would have been entirely different."

"But," Burge added, "one day, Hajdukovich will be gone and the Indians can not rely on one man always." He suggested more governmental involvement in the area. He pushed for a larger game reserve, which fueled the territorial ambitions of McIntosh and Dimler.

Agnes Abraham and Reverend E. A. McIntosh, c. 1939

Mission at Tanana Crossing

From the time, years earlier, when he first appeared as an itinerant Episcopalian, lay preacher at the Tanana Crossing mission, E.A. McIntosh was often in conflict with John. Back in 1912, McIntosh had supervised the Natives in the construction of the mission. At that time, he was quoted in the *Fairbanks Daily News-Miner* as saying, "The missionary is the father of the Natives and they obey his rulings. The chief and six counselors rule the village under the supervision of the missionary."

McIntosh and John approached the Natives differently. John knew that for the Indians to survive, the men had to trap, hunt, and chop wood daily. Their wives and children were critical to the enterprise.

The mission, however, mandated that the families stay near the mission for about seven months of the year. Thus, with the sons remaining at the church while their fathers were trapping, the sons did not learn the traditional subsistence methods. The Natives' fur harvest, and of course their profits, began to decline.

Not only did the new mission disrupt Native life, but according to Paul Kirsteatter of Healy Lake, McIntosh also opposed the Natives' potlatch traditions. Reportedly, he would burst through the door if he heard a potlatch was in progress and demand that it terminate.

Jerry Isaac, Tanacross Tribal Council President, 1998

Clothes were donated, according to Kirsteatter, to the church that were sold by the pastor, rather than being charitably dispensed, as originally intended. This story circulated so widely it was later reported by Rika's relatives in Sweden, the stories of "the pastor who sold the offering."

As the pastor reputedly began trading donated furs and goods, he asked John to transport his donated wares down the river. When John refused, McIntosh documented strong complaints against John in the federal public record.

Aggravating the situation, a new teacher, Fred A. Dimler, had replaced Jack Singleton as the Tetlin teacher. Dimler and McIntosh frequently were in a tug-of-war with John over which village, Tanana Crossing, Nabesna, or Tetlin, got the most governmental benefits. The territorial competition also resulted in the arbitrary currying of Native favor, for the purpose of achieving particular goals. Fighting for Tanana Crossing and against the exclusive Reserve, McIntosh wrote in 1931, "Mr. Hajdukovich is trying to depopulate the Crossing. Fine, if the Natives could be controlled from Tetlin, but there is an old feud and it would cause trouble if the people were thrown together."

Never Reimbursed

John told Mallinckrodt in 1941 that he would no longer deal with the Office of Indian Affairs. He said that, during just a few years, all of their twenty years of work had been undone. Additionally, John was so bankrupt he was forced to sell his business to Herman Kessler, the man who had first brought liquor to the Indians. In 1942, John went to Washington D.C., to the Office of Indian Affairs, seeking reimbursement for the money owed him from his stores. They promised him they would pay him at the end of World War II. In 1947, however, the O.I.A. disavowed ever having promised to help.

After the Alcan highway was built in 1942, the river traders became an anachronism. John's stores were a moot point. His life's work was, like his trading boat's name, a *White Elephant*, further aggravated by the reputed failure of all but one of the Native stores.

Unhappy with both the defunct vision and the divisive effect of the Tetlin Indian Reserve, John took steps for a legislative memorial, to have the Alaska State Legislature in Juneau reconsider the area's Reserve status.

It has been contended by some that John could have done more to elevate the Natives' interest over his own. As Jerry Isaac, Tanacross Tribal Council President remarked, "Business requires self-interest." Had John been more businesslike in his Upper Tanana trading, he might not have died twenty-three thousand dollars in debt, and something might then have been left for his daughter.

John had entered the North in 1904, at an opportune time. In 1939, that window closed forever. As he profited with opportunity, so John was also caught in a kaleidoscopic, social-political change far beyond his control. John was simply out of time and out of money.

The Native Under the Office of Indian Affairs/John's Retrospective

In 1948, John wrote to Mallinckrodt about the Office of Indian Affairs, "I am enclosing some correspondence with the O.I.A. You can see they don't want to do everything as they promised. Originally, they said they would do wonderful work at Tetlin and they made a great showing for the O.I.A. Of course at that time, they were willing to promise everything. I trusted them and their words. Nothing in writing has appeared now after almost ten years. They can see their failure and they are trying their best to smuggle themselves out without notice.

"Tetlin looks good, but the foundation for all that was laid by someone else and not by O.I.A.

"When we left there or better, that was when we were chased out of Tetlin by the Indian Office, there was a population there of over one hundred people: forty-five kids going to school. Twenty of them are in the graveyard now. Not because of distance, but because there is nobody left there…The O.I.A. will have to leave, too.

"It is not at Tetlin alone, but all over in good many places throughout the Interior. I made a trips a couple of years ago to Bering Sea and along the Kuskokwim. Same situation exists wherever one goes. The Indian Office throughout the Interior has done more harm to the Natives in a good many localities throughout the Interior.

"The Indian office failed to make white men out of the Natives and the Indian Office ruined Natives in a good many localities, so they are not Natives no more.

"There is good evidence in many places of Native kids dying. Spoonful of Castor oil would save their lives. And still, the Indian Office is getting large appropriations, of course through the support of many good citizens and good organizations.

"The Indian office has not shown test results to match the appropriation they

Federal Government In Competition With the Private Trader

From 1906 through the 1930s, the traders had been the connection between the Natives' subsistence culture and the white man's market, but those days were quickly fading.

In 1936, cheap credit was available to the Natives through the Alaska Reorganization Act. The subsequent loans to the Indians allowed them to compete directly with the traders. Although untrained in management, the Indians were encouraged to operate their own stores and to run a trading boat up the Tanana.

Chief Peter Joe of Tetlin began to build a wall against the "white trader." He organized a tribal council and procured a loan for a cooperative store and a freight boat.

Charlie David,
Tetlin elder, 1998

John Hajdukovich had spent his life protecting the Natives. He was also owed a great deal of money with no prospect of remuneration. John was further insulted by the new presence of Fred Dimler, the old irritation of E. A. McIntosh, and the new posture of Chief Peter Joe.

A wedge, "the carrot of self determination," began to be driven between factions supporting John and those favoring the position of Tetlin's Chief Peter Joe. The Chief called a Tetlin tribal meeting that "broke all hearts," Tetlin elder, Charlie

have been getting. Of course, along the Southeast coast, they have done a little because they have to put up some kind of a front to blind congressional parties and others who are interested in advancement of Natives of Alaska. I am not calling the Indian Office 'outlaws,' but they are not far from it.

"I remember reading in the magazine called, 'American Indians,' written by Eugene Kelly, analyzing people of Alaska. In every way being unfair in treatment of Natives of Alaska.

"Association of Indian Affairs very likely was of the same opinions because

David, remembered in 1998. In a four hour meeting, young Charlie was devastated by the tug-of-war between "Native management" and the betrayal of the gentle man who had always been a father. Although John was "allowed to remain in Tetlin," he could not run his business. According to Tetlin elder, Alfred John, John's Native friends attempted to re-pay some of the twenty three thousand dollar debt by giving him blankets and guns, but it was far from what was owed.

Enna Albert, Chief Walter Northway's daughter,1998

Charlie David was no longer able to endure anymore. He ran home and wept.

After the meeting, the Chief wrote to the Office of Indian Affairs accusing John of importing liquor and asking for his removal from the village where he had traded since 1918.

John had initially attracted governmental interest in the Natives' needs and was now caught on the point of his own sword. "Run out of Tetlin by the Office of Indian Affairs" was how John referred to it in a later letter to Mallinckrodt.

The battle, however, continued to rage, both at Tanana Crossing and Nabesna, as outside interests played the self-determination "card." McIntosh and Dimler encouraged Native leaders to testify: "Get John Hajdukovich out of the village." Enna Albert, Chief Northway's daughter, was asked why her father requested John's removal from Nabesna. Enna was puzzled. She said, "My Dad never understood why his friend, John, never even returned."

She added, "My Dad was an adult before he ever saw his first white man. I doubt he knew what he was attesting to in the public record. He missed John Hajdukovich. And, in 1950, he needed his help badly."

they allowed all that analysis to be written in their magazine.

"Eugene Kelly must be a good citizen, but with all that analysis on the white people of Alaska, and without foundation, it shows that Mr. Eugene Kelly is just the mouthpiece of the O.I.A.

"But if the O.I.A. and the supporters of that organization want to be fair, first to the white people of Alaska and to the Natives, they should send Mr. Eugene Kelly to Alaska to find out the truth and report, of course, the traveling. Inspection should be independent of the O.I.A., which they don't allow that if they can help it.

"I am not a journalist or writer and it's too late to try and be one, but as a citizen of Alaska, I did get a little hurt from that writing.

"I have lived up here for forty-six years and in all this time, I haven't seen no discrimination with Natives. When we first got here, the Natives took us for friendly. We accepted the Natives. Since then, we shared good and bad. The Natives done their share and we done ours and both are slaves to the bureau and not to Mr. Eugene Kelly. He states in his writing that the Natives are slaves to the white man."

In an aside, John confided, "The O.I.A. is worse than the natural predators the Natives trap."

In 1998, Jerry Isaac, Chief Isaac's nephew and Tanacross Tribal Council President, expressed opinions that concurred with John's observations. Very pensively, Isaac observed, "Before all the modern legislation and influx of money, Natives and whites in the Bush shared an intimate life together. They attended each others' dances, and felt free to drop in anytime at each others' homes. There was not today's artificial divide, which prosperity, urbanization, and big government have brought. Everyone was much closer. It was a nicer time."

As federal funds became available, the O.I.A. began to offer a marketing system to the Native, which drove a wedge in the trust between trader and villager that once had been whole.

High Dreams; Big Heart;
No Taste for Paperwork: Debt

"Never go into debt," John Hajdukovich advised the young prospector brothers, Carl and Oscar Tweiten, at the Big Delta roadhouse in 1933. "Whoever pays your bill controls your destiny," the trader said as he approached the rough waters of insolvency.

Ted Lowell said, "John never made any money." Lowell continued, "I'll tell you how it was. People showed up and John said, 'Come on in...' He just lost his shirt up there."

"John was good to all people," Carl Tweiten continued. "When anyone needed anything, they could go to his warehouse and get it. Sometimes they paid him back, but mostly they did not. John was always told what was taken." With all John's losses, Carl concluded, "John never sold any of his mining claims." He believed in it that much.

John's Family; Milo Marries in Montenegro

Godfather, Jelena Lesperovic, Milo Hajdukovic, Kolasin, Montenegro, 1935

In 1932, John wrote, perhaps for the first time, to his daughter, Andje. He sent a photo of the roadhouse to twenty-nine year old, Andje. He explained, "This was my house where I once thought we would come and live together as a family." Not mentioning that Milica refused to come, he continued, "But I sold that house."

In the letter, John wrote, "I would like to have a little talk with you, but do not tell anybody about it except Milica. I believe you will tell me the truth without any shame because I am your father and I need to know this. You are already getting older and I would like very much if you would get married.

"Before anything else, I would like to tell you this: when I got married, everybody was against it from my family side and they didn't agree that I marry Milica. The same was with her family. Nobody wanted her to marry me. Her brother said, 'If you marry him, you will beg on the street.' Maybe he guessed well! Only her mother was not against us. We were in love and married only because we loved each other. Because of this, Milica suffered a lot and how it was for me, I know the best.

"She raised you, not me, and I do not have right to expect from you answers to any of these questions I asked, but I am thinking about your well-being and your future. Is there any man whom you would like to marry? Or better to say, whom you love? Of course, he has to love you, too! And it does not matter if he has not even a verige ['vehr-eejg], [a Montenegrin hearth/a suspended pot above the cooking fire]. But he has to be honest.

"This is for your good and my biggest wish is for you to get married. It does not matter where he is from as long as he is not some uzma ['ooz-muh] [a person who is mentally and physically deficient].

"Will you tell me the truth when you respond to me? I never asked you before for anything, so I hope this time you will be truthful with me. I know I was young.

Ted Lowell, Tanana Crossing, c. 1930

With other young men and women, it was the same. Milica is now old and maybe she forgot that she was young, too.

"Maybe somebody who came from America is spinning the story that I have here property. Somebody could try to marry you thinking that he would get some money from me. That would be a really unhappy wedding."

(In 1998, this letter was found, incomplete, in John, Milica and Andje's now deserted home in Podgor-Utrg, Montenegro, in Andje's drawer.)

Milo and Jelena - 1935

At the time that John wrote this letter to his daughter, he was also encouraging his cousin, Milo, to marry. Milo was sixty and could finally offer a bride a comfortable life. Montenegrin culture assumed Milo would return home for a bride. An old friend of Milo's, Jovan Lesperovic ['Lespehr-vich], was the father of eight beautiful girls in Kolasin ['Koh-lahsheen], Montenegro.

In 1935, John put Milo on the Lockheed Electra airplane bound for the Balkans. For thirty-two years, Milo had not seen his father, Marko; brothers, Stanko, Mirko, Drago, Mico, and Filip; his mother, Miloslava; or his four sisters, Milica, Stanica, Katarina, and Ljubica ['Loo-beet-za]. After much crying and hugging, Milo attended that afternoon's "Korzo," ['Kor-zoh], that special promenade when young men and women parade up and down the street visiting each other. Milo saw the beautiful Kristina and Jelena ['Yel-enuh], two of Jovan Lesperovic's daughters. He sent word to Jovan that he wanted to meet with him at the local kafana [kuh-'fah-na], a bar, where men's business was transacted. After a few, hospitable brandies, Jovan's oldest daughter, Kristina, was promised to Milo. However, Kristina had other ideas. Jelena, though only fifteen, and at her father's urging, volunteered to marry Milo.

While the wedding was prepared, Milo took the train to Virpazar near Lake Skadar to see Milica and Andje in the mountains of Podgor-Utrg. Milica and Andje were dressed all in black and lived in the tiny rock room where John had been born, above the goat stall. Sustained by family, they eked out a living. Cousins, Jovan and Ilinka Hajdukovic, looked after the women, got their mail, and brought them groceries. The women agreed to attend Milo's wedding in Kolasin.

At a lavish wedding just four years before World War II ripped Yugoslavia apart, Milo and Jelena were married. On their way home to Alaska on a luxurious steamship, they mailed sophisticated photos of themselves to Fairbanks. Upon arrival, they were immediately welcomed into high society. "John," it was said in the *Fairbanks Daily News-Miner,* "got in his private car and went up the river to winter." Jelena became known in Fairbanks as "Ellen," and attended school with first grade children, so that she might learn English.

Transition to the Modern Age
Paternalism, or a Father? John's Heritage

In the newspaper, *Alaska Frontier*, John Hajdukovich was described in the 1940s as "a trader on the Tetlin Indian Reserve, but more than a trader, a father to the Tetlin Indian."

"My grandparents depended on John," Jerry Isaac, nephew of Chief Isaac, said. "He not only understood subsistence, but he tried to ready the Indian for change."

Weighing the paternalistic issue, Jerry Isaac said, "I credit the man for thinking these issues through. He was the lone guy who worried about the socio-economic life of the Native. He had a magnificent idea. I wish my grandparents had done that for me!"

"We have him to thank for pensions," Jerry continued. "Under the Social Welfare Act, our elders began getting fifteen dollars a month in pensions, due to John."

When Charlie David, a Tetlin elder, was asked if John were a guardian or a profiteer, he simply answered, "After the village meeting when Chief Peter preferred a Native store instead of the traders', we were encouraged to no longer sell to John."

Charlie continued, "Titus David, and I worked all summer with John expanding the village airstrip. Originally, there was sixty-five hundred dollars allotted for the project, but John had gone over the budget and was working on his own time… We figured it was good just to work with John. We never expected to get paid.

"But after the snow fell, one early winter evening, we heard a little plane coming in just under the clouds. Here come, that 'bad guy' with something in his hand. That 'bad guy,' he hand me and Titus what he say he gonna pay us. Is that this 'bad guy' we are talking about…?"

"Another time," he smiled, "a little baby got sick, real sick. We flew her out.

But we had to land on a sandbar cause it was fog and cliffs…but baby had mastoid infection…

"John came to us, and stayed all night. He make a fire, collecting firewood to keep us all going. Is this 'that bad guy' we talking about…?"

Charlie slowly continued, "You know, if you owed John money, he never ask for it. Never. He figure you…know. When you can, you will. He see you and just say, 'How you doing, Charlie?' He never embarrass anyone."

In John's old country, honor was more important than wealth. There were many sides to this honor, but it was believed if a man were vulnerable, he should be protected even from those with power. There, as with the Athabaskans, quality of life was esteemed more than gain.

As Charlie listened in 1998 to John's voice recorded on tape, a warm, nostalgic smile spread across his face.

"I miss him still…," Mary Gene, another Tetlin elder at the table, murmured.

As the Old Timers Die...

Emil Hammer, Found Frozen On the Trail...

One of John's wranglers, and a cook, Hughie Ross was found, by John, dead in his cabin in 1934.

Like an echo of the inevitable, Emil Hammer, one of the first on the Canyon Creek strike of 1913, and the last Healy River trader, prepared a strange farewell one day in 1938. He summoned the Healy Lake people together and began giving away the valuables from his store. Then, although it was -50° F., Hammer left with his sled, loaded with furs and a bottle of whiskey, pulled by only three dogs. When Hammer did not return home, Ted Lowell went looking for him. Down the trail, he found Hammer's mittens discarded. His frozen body was lying next to a stack of matches, with an empty whiskey bottle nearby. Down the trail, his few dogs were in a tangled mess. "It was strange," said Kathleen Newton Shafer, "because Emil never drank. He was a very nice man."

That winter of 1938, Lowell brought the prospector's body to McCarty. An old friend built the coffin. In the spring, Hammer was buried next to Hughie Ross on the Tanana's south bank, marked with a concrete cross.

For the next three years, Lowell took over Hammer's old Newton trading post. Lowell hauled 15 tons of freight for winter trade, according to the *Fairbanks Daily News-Miner of* August 16, 1938: "White Pendleton wool blankets and .30-.30 Winchester rifles were the standard articles of trade at Healy, also traps, gear for camp and trail, staple foods, mostly dried stuff, easy to pack." The article

Wedding of Milo Hajdukovic, the bald man in center rear, with his bride, Jelena Lesperovic seated, in white, with bouquet, 1935, Kolasin, Montenegro

continued, "Seems blankets are the Indians' equivalent of 'gilt-edge securities.' Each short line, or 'point' woven into a Point Blanket used to indicate the number of beaver pelts once exchanged for the blanket, effecting, of course, the size of the wool blanket purchased. In good fur years, Natives buy big Pendleton robes or Hudson Bay Company's 3 ½ or 4 point blankets. They buy more than they need, store them in their cache and in lean seasons, bring them in to the trader for credits. Blankets, not cash, are the trade basis. A standard white Pendleton blanket is 64 by 84 inches, weighs about 5 pounds and has a trade value of ten dollars."

A Promoter, Not a Miner
Tales of "Hajduk," the Prospector

Silas Solomon, 1927

Two young Norwegian brothers, Carl and Oscar Tweiten, were eager to mine and put in a new trail to Tibbs Creek off the Goodpaster River. John had all the excuse he needed, and in 1937, he followed the brothers with a large # 7 caterpillar, towing a sawmill. All his life, John never learned to operate a caterpillar, a truck, or any other equipment. Louis Grimsmore and "Doc" Cripes alternated running all of John's machinery. Some affectionately called Hajdukovich, "John, the Duke."

His large cat could go almost anywhere and that is where John directed it. In crossing a grassy lake once, Carl Tweiten recalled, "the cat hit a warm spot and sank into soft mud to the top of its tracks." John and his crew had to walk 30 miles back to town.

In Fairbanks, John saw the Tweitens and explained the problem. The brothers said they would take care of it. John, waving his hand, said he was sure their small cat could not extricate the large one.

However, when the brothers arrived in the swamp, they ingeniously devised a complicated system using dynamite, a "deadman," and wire rope. They blasted the larger tractor up by means of pressure, as well as using pulleys connected to the smaller caterpillar. Finally, both cats arrived up the Goodpaster. "Old timers," Carl said, "always helped each other with everything."

Carl continued in his book, *Alaska, Big Delta and the Goodpaster Region,* "One feat that John accomplished will not be duplicated.

"John's tractor had been left all winter up the Goodpaster. By late spring, he needed the tractor with 8 foot, spiked wheels, but it was sitting in the Goodpaster's flats near the lower south fork."

Tweiten explained, "The Big Delta Airfield was to be built, and Lytell and Green Construction Company were hiring the first one in with a large dozer.

"John and his crew started across the flats below the Volkmar River to the Tanana. John knew the Tanana and had a spot figured where there was a good bottom and it was shallow.

"The mechanics removed the fan belt and attached a pipe extension to the air intake. While crossing the tractor across the river, it became completely submerged, and continued going deeper until the water had almost covered the air intake pipe.

"When John saw the cat begin to crawl up the opposite shore, his face broke into a relieved smile like the sun.

"Whenever John told this story," Carl remembered, "he always excitedly waved his hands for emphasis."

Carl's stories of John abounded.

John and His Will Power

Carl Tweiten recalled that once when John was prospecting in the Alaska Range when the temperature was -50° F., he ran out of tobacco. Needing to satisfy his craving, he waded through icy overflow, deep water oozing over the fragile creek ice. The liquid ice seeped over his boot tops and filled his shoes. He finally stomped into the roadhouse angry with himself. "Any habit," he smacked his fist to the table, "that has such a hold that I'd a risk my life for… has a'gotta go!" That was the end of John's tobacco habit.

Flying with Culture

In the Balkans, there is contention between the Roman Catholics, who are western influenced, and the Eastern Orthodox. Those in the Eastern Orthodox faith are culturally different from Roman Catholics, and even cross themselves from another direction. Pat, one of the McCarty bachelors, was a Catholic. John was Orthodox. Pat was also nervous about flying.

One day, Pat and John flew into the Tweiten brothers' mining camp. As they took off, "Pat," John told Carl Tweiten "had a hard time holding onto the security strap while crossing himself at the same time!"

John's mining cat train, 1940

Miscoviches and Hajdukovich, Up the Goodpaster

John did nothing small. His hunting ventures in the 1920's had catered first class service to the wealthiest of America's new tourists. His trading employed "half the Natives in the Tanana valley," boosting the economy of the second largest river valley in the Alaskan interior.

In mining, John was no different. Fully confidant, John strode one day into the home of fellow Slav, Pete Miscovich, and skillfully persuaded him to invest in gold mining up the Goodpaster River.

John later described his biggest mining venture, whose failure greatly contributed to his financial breakdown.

John said very somberly, "I made a trip Outside. I got around twenty-five to thirty thousand dollars in freight, which included a complete outfit for six men for six months. Another thirty thousand dollars cash was set aside to pay those men.

In 1940, with a grub stake from Pete, John bought a top-of-the-line caterpillar. Then, with loaded metal sleds, called "go-devils," and wagons, John skidded his mining outfit to Central Creek, up the Goodpaster River. Silas Solomon, of Kechumstuk, freighted 24 tons of goods cross-country with the cat train. Natives, Kenny Thomas and Abraham Luke, drove 50 foot river boats, 80 miles up the Goodpaster River loaded with 7,000 feet of hydraulic pipe.

Where Lawrence and Walter Johnson had discovered coarse gold, John began open-cut, hydraulic mining.

There they worked until the money was exhausted, but the color never showed. After two such seasons, prospects looked grim. Pete Miscovich was stuck with the bill, and John with a crushing debt. John later summed it up, "Now, all I have left is a D-6 cat and," he added heavily, "my experience."

"He was a promoter, not a miner," Pete's son, Andy Miscovich said ruefully.

John's Statement on the Mineral Prospects of the Tanana Valley

John summed up the first fifty years of the prospectors' work in the Interior: "They discovered metals in hard rock: copper, nickel, antimony, mica, gold, tungsten, and even discovered platinum in a hard rock. Not very many places they discovered that peridot, but it's there.

"And even if only part of that was developed into mining, there is plenty there to support between thirty-five and forty thousand people.

"Sometime in the future," John prophesied, "the Goodpaster Trail and the branches leading out of the Goodpaster Trail, someday... will lead our younger generation to find natural success. Now, our main interest is not dead by a long way…but at a standstill due to obstacles."

In the late 1990's, one of the most promising gold deposits, albeit deep rock, not placer, was discovered on the Goodpaster near John's prospect. Rock at that depth can only be mined by modern mining equipment. Defying logic, John, a Balkan enigma, knew, somehow, the gold was there.

Rika's Roadhouse in the 1930s

Rika's Cuisine

Rika, c. 1930

Rika was a gol-durned independent woman," early Fairbanksan, Bob Redding explained, adding, "A roadhouse's success was based on an owner's personality. Rika was interesting to her friends, but she struck strangers as an oddity."

"Her place was an oasis to truckers, a respite for those freighting from Valdez to Fairbanks," Dick Osborne, the former owner of Alaska Tours, remembered fondly. "Mealtime was formal. If you weren't punctual, you had to settle for pie and coffee. Everything cost a dollar each: dinner, a room, coffee. Rika usually had a rabbit stew and giblet gravy on the wood stove for her guests."

Bob Redding remembered wryly, "The rabbits were so thick you could walk on their heads, and Rika shot them routinely. Some of us were glad when the rabbits died off!"

Delicate bear fat crusts filled with berries and served with milk from her springhouse made the meal complete.

Rika's fresh milk was a treat to the trappers, but getting the milk could be a challenge. Her free-ranging Holstein cattle mixed freely with marauding, stray buffalo.

Frequently, Rika asked Dick Osborne to crank up the Model A and accompany her for the nightly milking. Osborne stood watch for bison, while she set up her stool, bucket, and muslin cloth next to the cow, huddled in a grove of trees.

Maria Charlotta, Rika's sister, and Rika, 1932

Clabbered milk, slightly-spoiled fish, and rabbit dinners had long been the accepted fare for prospectors. This did not, however, suit the new tourists of 1939.

Rika did not have refrigeration, though electric lights were provided by her "one lung" generator.

Professionalism was necessary for the new tourist trade. The aroma of ripening cheeses around Rika's entry was not what Mr. Edgecumbe of Valdez' Golden Heart Stagelines desired. More importantly, he had to be confidant of his tourists' cuisine. Even though Rika was on the Board of Directors for the Richardson Highway Transportation Company, she did not adjust to the change that was coming.

In Fairbanks, Mr. Edgecumbe asked professional cooks, Bert and Mary Hansen, to build a place on the river bank opposite from Rika's, to cater to his tourists.

Consequently, from 1939-58, the Hansens ran a lodge on the Tanana's north bank, the other dock for the ferry.

"So, on both sides of the Tanana, roadhouse owners were then running an inn twenty-four hours a day. They were up at 4 A.M.: cooking and serving breakfast," remembered Bob Redding.

"After cleaning up from one meal, the linens all had to be hand washed and changed. Supper was ready on the dot at six."

Rika and Florence Allen Holmes

The years were taking a toll on the hard-working Rika. In the summer of 1938, she hired Florence Allen, a University of Alaska student, to help her with the cooking, baking, and cleaning.

Arriving before the spring ice was out, Florence rode across the icy Tanana in the tram bucket with mail carrier, Roy Lund, to begin working for Rika. Dangling her feet, she skimmed above the water to Rika's south bank.

Florence was the second girl who had worked for Rika, but unlike the first, Jean Hunter, she refused to learn to milk!

Like a daughter, Florence followed Rika around. The two got along well and Rika confided some in Florence. Fussing once about people pandering to her in hopes of inheriting the roadhouse, Rika smiled knowingly to young Florence saying, "But we both know who will receive my inheritance…"

When Florence was asked if there might ever have been anything romantic between John and Rika, she responded, "…Well, I don't even remember seeing John. I don't think so.

"The one Rika seemed to light up around was Louis Grimsmore. I always thought she liked him."

In response to whether there might ever have been "any girls" hustling a business on the property, Florence knew nothing about it.

When Carl Tweiten was asked his opinion of John and Rika's relationship, he said simply, "Well…they were young, once…" Carl could not resist adding that when Rika's sister, Maria, was visiting her in 1932, he remembered the girl talk he overheard between the two sisters. "Conversation," he said, "they thought I didn't understand." But the spicy, veiled conversation remained in the young man's mind well into his nineties.

Rika did write a letter to John on one of his many trips into the Bush. She caught him up on the news about Butch and Carl Armstrum, as well as the farming news: the growth of the grain, a loose cow. Finally, she cautioned him "to be careful," and noted she was sending some bran doughnuts to him up the river. To others, she said proudly, "The man never gits too old to go into the hills."

Rika's 1938 Trip to Sweden

Rika's sister, Maria Charlotta, died in the fall of 1932, after their last visit. Facial expressions in the photos from that last visit seem to indicate both sisters knew Maria was not at all well.

After Maria died, Rika wrote to their remaining family in Sweden, "There is no inheritance. For that, you'll have to wait until I die."

Five years after Maria Charlotta's death, Rika visited her brother, Carl's, surviving family in Minnesota. She enjoyed it so much that she spontaneously got on a plane and returned to Sweden. However, she had not time to apprise herself of current fashions. Her wardrobe dated to the beginning of the twentieth century! Rika thought Victorian, street-length clothes cinched in with a corset were still high fashion. When she arrived in Sweden dressed in an outrageous purple hat, matching dress, and stockings, her seventeen year old niece, Britta Gellert, was mortified.

Rika spent two months with her family, visiting from house to house at Lake Tysslingen. In Sweden, the invitation to visit meant literally, "Come, see how we live," denoting a people proud of their cakes and china. The decorum was a marked departure from Rika's Alaskan life of shooting rabbits and feeding unkempt trappers.

Stockholm, the jewel of the Baltic Sea, was a world away from Big Delta on the Tanana River.

One day, Rika must have had enough of "the dainties." She and the other ladies had been consigned to a bedroom for the daily nap. At the appropriate hour, Rika's niece opened the door carrying a tray of cookies and porcelain. As the door began to open, Rika aimed with her slipper. Confidently, she let fly at the door jamb, smacked it and narrowly missed hitting Britta's head and the fragile cups. Rika had had enough. It was time to return to dodging the wandering buffalo in Big Delta.

When she arrived home to Big Delta, she found that Marnie Washburn, the young man whom she had left in charge of the roadhouse, had left it a catastrophe. The sheep were dead, he had harvested the wrong crop, and he had burned some of her hand-woven cane chairs. Rika vowed never, ever…to leave again.

In 1952, however, Rika's youngest brother, Jakob, returned the visit and traveled across the Atlantic to see Rika.

Early Alaska Trucking

The Richardson Road

In 1922, the Alaska Road Commission published a guidebook for the Richardson Road, formerly the Valdez-Fairbanks Trail. It was an effort to encourage tourists to try the 386 mile raw road, despite that travelers had to pack a shovel to make gravel ramps at creek banks for stream crossings, as well as push their vehicles uphill.

Nonetheless, the guidebook advertised the trail's roadhouses, showing a photo of "John's roadhouse" with the accompanying text, "M'Carty's Roadhouse. John Hajdukovich, Propr…Accommodates 40 people. Meals $2; Beds $1; Guides, $7.50 per day…boat…Pack horses…"

Early Alaskan Trucking

In the late 1920s, Gene Rogge fired up his wooden-spoked, one-ton Chevy pickup for his first Valdez-to-Fairbanks run. He was one of several kids fresh out of high school who were freighting goods from Valdez to the Interior, including Al Ghezzi, Jess Bachner, and Charlie Simmons. Routinely, they faced overflow, whiteouts, open rivers, and failing cars—everything, but federal controls.

Alaska, which was nicknamed, "the Attic that Uncle Sam built," was, in 1941, being manipulated by its landlord. The federally subsidized railroad was failing. To save it, the federally run Alaska Road Commission began to manipulate the playing field. The A.R.C. directed freight bound for Fairbanks to go via the railroad, rather than by the independent truckers. To push truckers out, the A.R.C. began charging a toll for the McCarty ferry. For commercial freight loads, the cost was $9.27 a ton. But, to attract railroad business, the railroad lowered its freight costs. It was too much for the truckers. "Doc" Gordan, the head of the Alaska "gypo" (a term first used for subsistence level, Oregon logging, early truckers) truckers, met the A.R.C. head-on. Using his truck, he blocked access to the Big Delta ferry. The other truckers immediately followed suit. Using a gun in a half-serious way, Gene Rogge and Charlie Simmons tied up the ferry pilot. Later, Rogge smiled, "No jury in Fairbanks would have convicted us. We were the hometown boys bringing affordable groceries home."

In the following months, the truckers built their own ferry, flew a pirate flag, and continued to freight. A little gas launch, the *Paul Bunyan,* pushed the barge across the river, flying a skull and crossbones.

The rebellion, however, was later put to rest by Hitler's chaos in Europe. In 1942, the United States Army began building the new military road, the Alcan Highway. The routing included the construction of a bridge across the Tanana River at Big Delta. Once the steel-span bridge was built, it replaced the McCarty/Big Delta's ferry and its tram car. Overnight, a way of life disappeared. The leisurely winters of Alaska's roadhouses evaporated like a chinook wind blowing through a forest. The modern age had come to the Interior.

John, far right, sawmill operation, Tok River, c. 1941

World War II

Hitler's March Across Sweden;
The Near Annihilation of Yugoslavia.

As Hitler began to march across Sweden and into Norway, John and Rika listened intently to the radio, catching the European news. When Serbia refused to co-operate with the occupying Nazis, all of Yugoslavia dissolved into flames and chaos. To punish the Serbian impudence, Hitler carpet-bombed Belgrade and its environs. The devastation was followed by civil war as Utashe, Croatian nationalists/Axis sympathizers, liquidated the so called undesirable. As the chaos escalated, thousands of Jews, Serbs, and Roma (Gypsies) were transported to the infamous Jasenovac Concentration Camp, "Croatia's final solution." Belgrade became Hitler's dumping ground for south Serbian Jewish corpses. Marshall Josif Broz Tito's communist Partisans promoted themselves as the country's only hope; they fought not only the Utashe, [Oo-'stah-shee] but also the betraying monarchists who had surrendered to Hitler. Those who did not support the Communists, like Milo's brothers, were marched out, their lands seized, and they were shot. Revenge was finally squelched as Tito, in 1945, consolidated the fragmented Kingdom of Serbs, Croats and Slovenes into a new Yugoslavia, ostensibly dedicated to "unity and brotherhood."

At home in Alaska, while personal communication with Yugoslavia was impossible, Chicago's *Serbian Unity* newspaper helped to keep John and Milo informed. At Fairbanks' Model Café, Serbs, Montenegrins, and Croats all studied the papers, discussing their birthplace, and the chaos engulfing it.

The Russian Lend Lease Program in Alaska

Just across the Bering Sea, Russian Slavs, a little closer to Alaska than Yugoslavia, were partnering with the U.S. Army to fight Hitler. A string of air bases had just been built across Alaska. These air bases were used for re-fueling airplanes bound for Russia, and the bombing of the eastern Axis front. Soviet pilots flew these Russian-leased, American planes from the U.S. to the U.S.S.R.

Left behind at Delta's new Allen Army Airfield were the Russian's hob nailed boots and their empty bottles of vodka.

The Rise and Fall of John's Sawmills

For the construction of the Alcan international highway, thirteen sawmills began operating from the Alaskan-Canadian border to Big Delta.

John owned three of the thirteen mills. To obtain 50,000 board feet of Gerstle River timber, John deposited fifty dollars for a grant, and installed a mill at the Gerstle. With a contract for 250,000 board feet, he put a second mill at the Tok River. Army engineers rented his sawmills, tractor, poling boat, and outboard. The soldiers floated the felled logs downstream, using John's boat to nudge them along to the sawmill. After the logs were milled into lumber, the Army used the boards to ticky-tacky the raw roadside with little shelters that were used for the bridge construction all the way to the Alaskan-Canadian border. John positioned his last mill at Hansens' Hollow, at the north end of the new Tanana River bridge.

Like Murphy's Law, John's cat broke when he needed it most. But the handy Tweiten brothers saw John sitting dejectedly by his broken caterpillar. John had a mess of cat "puzzle pieces" soaking in a detergent barrel. In a few hours, using their Nordic ingenuity, Carl and Oscar Tweiten had John's cat chugging across the new Tanana River bridge.

John knew as much about record keeping as he did about mechanics. To collect his money from the military, John's men were supposed to tabulate all the board feet that they sold to the Army. In John's Montenegro, not even land and marriage records were routinely documented on paper. John had not been raised to maintain a paper trail. When he was later asked about his sawmills' records, he simply responded, "Oh, I don't know. I never kept track of that." Those supervising John's mills never bothered either. Without the appropriate documentation at the project's end, the Army refused to pay John. For the last time, John lost a small fortune.

The Isolation of the Upper Tanana

Greater than all the previous gold rushes, World War II ushered a billion dollars into the territory. Alaska's ice-box isolation was converted overnight into a G.I. camp. During the summer of 1940, tons of construction materials were freighted to the Interior as military airfields and bases were built. The new Alcan trail connected Alaska, through Canada, with the lower 48 states.

Jovan and Ilinka Hajdukovic, support to MilicaAndje Hajdukovic, Podgor-Utrg, Montenegro, FRY, 1998

Patriotism was high. Natives from Nabesna to Tanana Crossing supported the U.S. Army building the international highway. When journalist Maury Smith traveled to the Upper Tanana that summer of 1940, he said, "Nabesna Indians live probably the purest form of Native life of any in the territory, uninfluenced by white man's habits." He added, "The federal game preserve, where only they are allowed to trap, protects Tetlin's forty-five people as well as shielding the one hundred people in Tanana Crossing."

Chief Peter Joe granted access to the Army Corps of Engineers through the Tetlin Reserve. Tanana Crossing patriotically supported the new international corridor directly through "their front yard." The Alcan's construction meant the end of Upper Tanana isolation.

In 1939, John predicted that a large military base would be built near Nabesna. Two years later, it was a fact. Nabesna evolved into the highway community that developed around the Northway airfield. Tanana Crossing and Tetlin were also eclipsed by the highway junction town of Tok.

In three years, Alaska was transformed from a dogsled trail to a graded corridor. Anyone with a little gas money, a vehicle, and permission from the military could travel. Overnight, traders became an anachronism.

Epidemic torched the isolated Native life as they mixed with white soldiers. White men's diseases ran unabated up and down river, invading every cabin, touching every person.

It was too late before a doctor sledded into the remote Healy Lake. Houses were filled with the dead, necessitating fast, shallow graves.

The sick sat in the supposedly, purifying steam bath, which, in reality, only spread the disease faster to the healthy. Those who escaped fled up the river.

John Hajdukovich said that in 1939 there were seventy-five children at Healy Lake. By 1943, so many children had died that a school was no longer needed.

Chief John Healy took his remaining children to the new highway. He desperately wanted a school. He thought he might have more chance of one being built if his family lived on the new highway, so he purchased a cabin at the Little Gerstle River where a small community began to form.

Adults: Peter and Sarah Thomas. Back right, Kenny Thomas, Mansfield, Alaska, c. 1938

Milo's Investments and the Death Years

Milo Hajdukovic, Gerstle River sawmill, c. 1941

When Milo left the Tanana in 1932, he sold his trading posts to John. Later, according to John, there was an agreement between the two of them that the money John had paid Milo for the stores was to be re-invested for them both in Fairbanks' property. Milo had already begun investing in Fairbanks' residential property. His business intuition was good, but it was refined and directed by banker, Ed Stroecker, lawyers, and businessmen. They urged him to invest in commercial real estate. The result was immediate rich gains.

At lunchtime, Milo could be seen walking the Fairbanks' streets evaluating real estate. He owned Fairbanks' finest restaurant, the Model Café with partners, George and Steve Bojanich, also Montenegrin. One of Milo's coups was a commercial building at Fourth and Cushman, in the heart of downtown Fairbanks, which he purchased for sixty thousand dollars. Busy with business and raising a family, Milo saw less of John.

In 1938, perhaps lonesome for the old life, Milo briefly returned to fur trading. He introduced his wife, Ellen, and their new daughter, Mary, to the Upper Tanana. Even today, Native elders remember that visit.

Ellen learned enough English, so that when her children, Mary and John, were seven and five, she landed a job at the new Ladd airfield.

Although Ellen was young, she was not completely well. Milo was not well at all. Although he did not advertise it, he had made a couple of trips to Mayo Clinic.

Ellen, however, neglected to see a doctor. According to her close friend, Vuka Stepovich, Ellen's problems should have been tended sooner.

In 1944, the beautiful, young Ellen was dead. Milo asked his boyhood friend, Charlie Miller, born Ilija Milajic, to move from Juneau to Fairbanks to care for Mary and John.

Later, Mary recounted that Milo was accustomed to setting the tone: Montenegrin style, when he entered any of his saloons. He set his pistol on the bar, and then proceeded with business. According to Mary's "Uncle" John's documentation, recorded at the University of Alaska archives, an argument developed in 1945 at Charlie Miller's rented bar, the Silver Dollar, between Charlie and Milo. Milo demanded the rent for the bar in front of Charlie's customers, which embarrassed Charlie. Charlie became angry, but Milo only responded, "You are talking to a dead man."

The next morning, although Milo did not feel well, Milo seemed intent, according to John, on moving his children. As he headed to his children's school, he agreed to stop only briefly at George Bojanich's for coffee.

As he sat in a chair waiting on the Bojaniches to prepare the beverage, Milo quietly died in the living room.

No one can tell a story as well as a Montenegrin. They are renowned for their expression, and John was no exception. On the legal record, John documented his view of the events surrounding Milo's death.

In a letter addressed to attorney E. B. Collins, John implied that Collins, without official authorization (but escorted by Mrs. Miller), entered Milo's house and obtained both sets of Milo's keys. John stated that Collins intimidated Jack Buckley, U.S. Deputy Marshall, to get the authority from the U.S. Commissioner for Buckley, Collins, and the bank representative to enter Milo's house.

With the permission secured, the three entered the house. John said Collins reached over into Milo's satchel of papers and just happened to extricate Milo's will. John commented, "Funny. According to Mrs. Miller, that wasn't there the day before."

John stated, "I been Milo's closest and only relative in this country, or any country, outside of his brothers and sisters." The banker "and the rest of you arranged in the will, supposedly signed by Milo, that to be the end of my relation with Milo's kids. I hear from the others that Milo left a will."

He continued, "I met" the banker "several times, he didn't even spoke to me. I met you on the street several times. Each time, you went by, didn't see me. On Wednesday, October 9th, I called your office and talked to you and told you that I am planning on leaving town next day and that I understand Milo left will. I would like to see the will and where is the place to see it. You told me, 'Come up to my office in a few minutes.' I got there. Mrs. Brown, your secretary, brought the will and handed it to me and stood alongside of you. I read the will and after I got through, I told you this will will be contested. You replied, 'By who?' 'By his brothers and sisters, but if his brothers are not alive, I contest it myself.' Then you started to tell me all the good points about the will.

"I told you I had an agreement with Milo. You and the bank have possession of Milo's house. 'Would you let me go with you and the bank representative to Milo's house to locate our agreement. It was there a month ago, just before I left for the Upper Tanana.' You answered, 'We are not quite ready to go through the papers, but you can be sure as soon as we go through the papers, we will let you know.'

"I added, 'Do you know, Mr. Collins, that I laid the foundation for that estate and worked for it for thirty years.' You affirmed this.

"You know, Mr. Collins, I have been waiting since October 9, 1945 and this is February 1958. I think I waited a long enough. Is time to get the reply.

"In 1946, I put in application in the commissioner's court asking to be appointed as guardian of Milo's children. Commissioner appointed me and I was to put $60,000 worth of bonds. We arranged for the bonds with the Alaska Insurance Agency. Next morning, I left for Kuskokwim. Several days later, I received a letter from Mr. Hurley that the bank objected to my appointment as a guardian of Milo's children. Lady commissioner revoked my appointment and appointed First National Bank of Fairbanks. Mr. Hurley advised me to return in Fairbanks, which I did. Mr. Hurley took it up in commissioner's court. I was listening to the proceedings. Mr. Clasby made the statement to the court, 'John Hajdukovich is not qualified to be the guardian of Milo's children.'

"I never can forgive Mr. Clasby for that statement. Milo's children, their father and mother are dead. Now my children, my name, and my blood.

"Of course, Clasby was instructed by the banker and you.

"The kids was stolen from me. That was the crime. Where were you, Mr. Collins. You didn't show up at the trial. You supposedly were my attorney by promise for life.

"All of you, especially" the banker, "was interested in the money he was going to get out of the estate and not in the children."

After Milo was buried at Birch Hill cemetery in an Elks' plot, John left for the Kuskokwim River. Some of the Hajdukovich kinsmen were fur traders and merchants on the Kuskokwim River, south of Fairbanks. Nikola Mihaljevic [Mee-'hal-je-vich] known as "Nick Mellick," was originally from a Montenegrin village near John's home. On the third largest river in the Interior, the Kuskokwim, Nick was also a store owner and fur trader. Wanting to discuss Milo's death with other countrymen, John and Nick traveled to Napaimute [Nuh-

'pie-myut] to see Pete Mihailovich [Mee-'hy-loh-vich], and to Aniak ['An-ee-ak] to visit Sam Voich ['Voy-eech].

Feeling reinforced, John returned to the Interior for a second trial. In his continued letter to his lawyer, Mr. Collins, John wrote, "I lost. I wasn't present at the agreements between Mr. Hurley and Mr. Clasby. Mr. Hurley told me he lost on a technicality. I believe there was crime connected with this. And someday, I prove to Mr. Clasby that technicality can never cover stains of crime.

"I wanted to appeal the case to the district court. But Hurley informed me that we have to have $250 cash. I took the money, but they changed their mind. Hurley told me that I have to have two bondsmen. So I got two bondsmen and they signed the bonds for me. I waited several days. Finally, I went to see Mr. Hurley and he told me they won't accept on the grounds that I had no authority to appeal the case.

"'Why you didn't tell me I could [had to] prove that I had authority?' 'Can anything be done?' I asked Hurley. Reply was, 'No, you just have to wait until the kids get of age.'"

John continued to Collins, "I waited for you to produce the agreement I told you about I had with Milo. I wasn't financially in the position to fight any further. My copy of the agreement I couldn't locate at that time and the one I sent to my daughter is in the old country since 1926. Same year it was agreed and here it is Mr. Collins. I want to read it to you."

The Agreement

"This agreement is made between John Hajdukovich of Big Delta, Alaska and Milo Hajdukovich of the same place on the 14th day of May 1926. John agrees to let Milo have full possession of John's trading post at Nabesna village, Upper Tanana with all the dry goods, groceries, hardware. Cash money taken by Milo from John to date, full amount of $22,000. Twenty two thousand dollars Milo is to trade at John's trading post at Nabesna village until 1931 with the following understanding: all the money accumulated by Milo's name with John's above investment [$22,000 from John]. John is to share and share equally with Milo in all the real estate property and personal property which is or will be in Milo's name in any part of Alaska after this date.

"It is further understood and agreed by Milo that he, Milo, is to never sell, dispose of, give away or will any of the property in his name or any part of it until mutually agreed with John in writing.

"Last that remains alive is to be the trustee, administrator for the deceased and to serve without bond or hold the estate to the best of his judgment. John's daughter in Montenegro, Yugoslavia is to be the beneficiary of John's share, but after all debts of John's are paid. And Milo's brothers or closest relatives are to be the beneficiary of Milo's share of the estate. Dated at Nabesna village this 14th day of May 1926. Milo Hajdukovich, John Hajdukovich."

Both signatures appear to be made by the same person. The paper is not witnessed or notarized.

John also wrote on a scratch paper the transactions between him and Milo dated Big Delta, Alaska, October 1945. It referred to mutual outstanding accounts between the two cousins, including even cancelled checks from Seattle Fur Exchange, dating from when Milo went to Yugoslavia in 1935.

In a correspondence with hunting client and attorney, John K. Howard, Boston, Massachusetts, dated July 27, 1950, Howard referred to John as having been close to insolvency in 1932. He said John had even approached his hunting clients, Endicott and Mallinckrodt, for loans.

Further, Howard recalled evidence John had told him in 1932, relevant to Milo's business. Howard wrote, "During these conversations, you told me that you did not believe that you could make a success of trading on the Upper Tanana unless Milo was eliminated from trading on the river, and that Milo had offered to sell out to you. You proposed to buy out Milo's boats, trading posts, caches, trade goods, and accounts receivable at Tetlin, Nabesna and Tanana Crossing for $25,000.00, part cash, notes for the balance. You also stated that Milo's business was a profitable business.

"It seemed peculiar to me that a man should want to sell a profitable business unless he was getting a fairly high price for it. In examining this point, you told me that you thought that Milo was not in debt except that possibly he might owe something on five thousand dollars' worth of goods, which had been shipped from Seattle and Tacoma to him recently and which you thought were at the villages in the Upper Tanana, but that he had furs with the supply houses who had furnished these goods worth at least the amount of the debt, if not more. You said that Milo owed a mortgage of $10,000 on a building in Fairbanks and that he also had perhaps $6000-$7000 in furs and credit from the sale of furs.

"You explained Milo's willingness to sell to you by saying when Milo first came to the Tanana to trade, he made a written agreement in 1922 with you whereby he agreed to leave at the end of two years. He also agreed not to put a gas boat on the Tanana. You said Milo had broken this agreement as to both those details. You protested against Milo in 1924, staying after two years. Milo stated

Fairbanks, Alaska, Slavic wedding: L-R: Mrs. & Mr. Charlie Miller (born Ilija Milajic) with Mary & John Hajdukovich, the children standing far left, c. 1946

that he had extended credit to the Indians and wanted another year to collect the credit. You agreed to let him stay on another year.

"In 1925, Milo put a gas boat on the river and also bought houses where he put trading posts in each of the three villages. You protested this. The nearest thing to any formal action taken by you upon this agreement was this summer when you had Milo sit down with you and District Attorney Hurley. Before Hurley, you told the whole story and protested against Milo not having lived up to his agreement.

"It is questionable whether such an agreement restricting a man from following any particular employment for an indefinite period, even in a restricted area, is enforceable at law either by a suit for damages or in equity for specific performance.

"There is also the question as to whether John has not waived any legal rights that he had under such an agreement.

"John feels that Milo offered to sell out his outfit to him either because he was afraid of his position under this agreement, or else because he felt that he had done wrong and wished to make amends."

Attorney Howard saw no motive for Milo to sell. Additionally, he saw discrepancies in John's narratives, pointing out quite strategically that in 1932 John told Howard that Milo owned a ten thousand dollar mortgage on Fairbanks' property, free and clear. Had Milo owed John, Milo's mortgage would not then have been stipulated as free and clear.

Additionally, John's communications to everyone regarding the business was not consistent. Howard pointed out that in John's submitted list of assets in 1932, there was no mention of shared real estate holdings with Milo in Fairbanks.

Howard concluded that relevant to any further legal proceedings any of John's 'evidence' would only potentially damage his case.

Among John's papers, there is an agreement relevant to the proceeds of the sale of Milo's trading posts, supporting John's contentions. It was signed by Milo and dated February 5, 1932. Plausible witness signatures were affixed from both Jack Singleton and Jack Yarich, but it was not notarized.

Among John's letters to his daughter in Montenegro, the agreement between him and Milo, which John claimed to have sent, was not found.

There was, however, a letter written to Andje from John, January 5, 1951, in which he explained Milo's death, as well as John's assets. By apology, John began his overdue letter to his daughter, "In your registered letter, I believe that you are wondering that I do not write and I will state here why if you want to believe.

"From that day, Milo and Jelena came back to Yugoslavia, everything turned bad with me and I lost almost everything I had. For this little what is left, I think that I will improve, but it is very uncertain. Some real estate which I now have is today under present condition, almost worthless. I never had cash money because everything was spent on maintenance of property, which was on Milo's name for which I paid the loan.

"When Milo died, he left a will in which property was left to children through one bank as a custodian. I was not mentioned in his will. I was very far, about 300 miles away. Milo was sick for a long time. He had some kind of seizure, which I knew, but hid, so nobody else would know.

"Jelena died in 1944 and Milo in 1945. Those people to whom he left in trust property and children knew in what condition he was and that he was not going to live too long, according to the doctor's statement. They used the opportunity and made his will according to their wish, which Milo signed.

"I went to court twice and lost both times. I will try once more, but now I don't have no money.

"Money which I sent last spring was borrowed. If I knew that you can send food over there, I would do that, but I will try to do that as soon as I can. Hope it is not going to be too late for you.

"Is Milica now really old and what was the problem with your health? What doctor said?

"So much for now and I will write again.

"Andje, I will send you one letter, so that you know contract between me and Milo. Maybe it will be for some use to you if you live long, but for Milica it is too late. Greetings, Jovo"

Three of Milo's brothers who were alive prior to 1945, were mentioned in the will: Filip, Mirko and Mico. The same year Milo died, three of his brothers and a nephew, all land-owners, were shot by the communists.

Until at least 1948, communication between Yugoslavia and the United States was very difficult. Yugoslavia had been reduced to rubble and converted to a Stalinist-aligned communist state. Confusion, and the cold war, reigned between the two countries.

John's wife, Milica, lived thirteen more years after the 1951 letter; Andje lived another twenty-three. Dying as paupers, they were buried in the same ground vault with their cousin, Stefan Hajdukovic. In the Hajdukovic church cemetery, clinging to the mountain ledge, Milica and Andje were laid to rest.

John's fate was no better. When he died in 1965, his friend, Fred Cook, scaled the Birch Hill cemetery fence in Fairbanks to honor him, and installed his friend's headstone.

Sometimes it is said of Slavs that they make no plans for tomorrow. In this, John, who planned for the Natives' old age, did more for them than he did for himself. Just before Milo left Big Delta in 1932, he reputedly demanded of John, "I've got mine. Do you have yours...?!"

The Last Days in the Roadhouse

Where there were bachelors, there were stills. For the prospectors, Pat Doherty made the best moonshine around. But, he was not alone. Rika always harvested spring's wild rose buds for jelly, as well as dandelions for wine. The truckers joked that Rika's wine was about 150 proof. Rika insisted her guests always have a full glass. "I could hardly walk afterward," Dick Osborne remembered with a laugh.

Capitalizing on the military camped near the bridge construction in 1942, Rika operated a package liquor store in the roadhouse. "Eight dollars a pint or fifteen dollars a fifth, whatever she could charge is what she got," Ted Lowell remembered.

There was talk, however, that she was raped by a soldier. Fearing for her safety, Rika stretched a chicken wire partition between her parlor and the kitchen. She hid the liquor in her bedroom until she made a sale.

When statehood invalidated Rika's cheap territorial liquor license, she, the previous babysitter for Bill Egan, reportedly called Governor William Egan at his mansion in Juneau, and demanded, "Give me 'Billy boy!'" After a few words

John and Rika c. 1965

with Egan, Rika kept her territorial liquor license.

Shuffling on arthritic, swollen ankles, Rika relied on others to keep her generator going. She had a favorite soldier who started the light plant. Every morning, he was rewarded with coffee and delicate, bear-fat pastry.

In 1947, when Rika retired as the postmistress, she converted the post office into a package liquor store.

During the day, she and John lived in the living room and the dining room. When new neighbors visited, Rika pointed out, "John lives here…but *he sleeps* there…," pointing to his shed behind the roadhouse.

If a deliveryman arrived, he had to holler to get Rika's attention. He was sure she was deaf. However, Rika's hearing was selective. "She heard what she wanted to hear," Milo's son, John, said. "When she didn't want to hear, she was stone deaf."

She almost did not hear her brother, Jakob, when he arrived at her front door in 1952. After the long trip, Jakob had caught a ride to Big Delta from Fairbanks. When he knocked at her roadhouse door, she greeted him with, "Oh, you're here?"

After another visitor, an aspiring prospector, arrived from home, Rika assigned him to milk cows and pitch hay. Pretty quickly disgusted, Ekstrom declared, "Rika was as uncivilized as the landscape."

Reaching for Straws

"...Sixty Six, No Trading Posts, No Cash, No Credit, No Driver's License"

After a lifetime of freighting, John had nothing to show for it, but the affection of many Native friends. He wrote to Senator Bob Bartlett asking for help to get reimbursement for his stores. Grasping for other solutions, he asked a Yugoslav distributor for Odom Liquor Company if he might distribute Budweiser beer, but nothing came of it.

However, between 1945-1955, construction in Alaska boomed as miliary bases were established. The burgeoning Allen Army/"Big Delta" Air Field and the Alcan Highway triggered the birth of Delta Junction, nine miles south of Big Delta.

As the Big Delta airfield grew, John worked for Lytle and Green Construction Company. He told a story of handling a sixty-four hundred dollar well-driller for them.

In a disjonted description of the drill breaking, John said he was then offered a military drill to use. He pushed the temptation aside, but he turned and gazed at the hundreds of Army tents pitched on either side of his old trading route. He murmured to himself, "I just don't want to see anymore."

In 1946, John rode a military bus from the Big Delta Airfield, up his old trail, to Tanana Crossing, arriving in only a matter of hours.

John agreed to help with the construction of the village's new airstrip, another encroachment of the modern age. He tried to pull his life together by stocking an abandoned Army building for a new store.

L-R: Jakob Jakobsson, Rika's brother; Rika Wallen; & two unknown men at her roadhouse, 1952

113

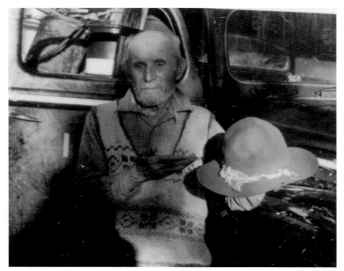

Hearing the news, a young child, Jerry Isaac, heard the cry, "The old man is back!" ringing through the village. The boy wanted to see the famous trader for himself, so he stepped shyly into John's slab warehouse. In a musical voice, the silver-haired Montenegrin waved to him, "Come on in...!"... as he had before to so many.

John's Christmas card to former clients, c. 1951

Silas Solomon First Saw John Trading in 1915 and Prospected With Him During the Last Days...

Silas Solomon was one of the last Natives raised at the old telegraph station of Kechumstuk. When he was young, he had piloted John's boats, wrangled horses, driven the caterpillar, and always, chauffeured John. In the late 1930s, he freighted 24 tons of pipe cross-country to Central with the Miscovich cat train.

During the same time period, Silas married. In 1939, their daughter, Irene Arnold (neé Solomon), was born. Tragically, Irene's mother died only two years later of a bad flu.

In 1998, Irene recalled, "Dad and John were gone together all the time." She added, "John was the only white man who was like family in our home. He taught me to make fish hooks and to use my imagination."

"My Dad did, too. He always said, 'Follow your instincts. You are probably a very smart person. Everyone is.'"

When John could no longer pay, Silas still chauffeured John. Together, they explored the Jarvis Creek coal fields and the Fortymile River country. They rambled the country. Nothing was an obstacle. They built bridges across flooded creeks, fixed busted radiators, and charged gas at the Fortymile Roadhouse. When Silas hung out with friends, John waited. During the 1950s, Silas drove the caterpillar with John across the treeless swamps to Ketchumstuk. With ½ inch, hand-made dowels, they marked the trail. For thirty hours, John, Silas, "Old Thomas;" his son, Will; and Fred Demit trudged across the muskeg and black spruce forest. Once there, John left for posterity a Cyrillic newspaper from home…just to make people think the "Russians had been there."

Silas said, "John always kept a bottle of Scotch in his dog sled bag. But he never tempted others with it." Silas added, "He got lonely. So did Rika." Remembering some detail, Silas hastily protested, "John was too protective of Rika!"

Into the mining country of Devil's Mountain, Slana, and Nabesna, and across the border into Canada, Silas drove John, looking for a theoretical "lost Klondike." The story went that two prospectors had once hit the "mother lode" there on their way to the Yukon, but when they returned to find it, they could not. John meant to find it.

Like a magnet, John was also drawn to a volcanic crater supposedly laced with nickel, but the crater was only accessible from the Johnson River. When he was seventy-six, on a trip trying to access the deep hole, John overnighted in his dog sled. During the night, snow buried the thin canvas covering John. In the morning, as soon as they could unfold their stiff, cold limbs, they tried to lower themselves into the hole. They stretched with ropes and even, a ladder, but to get a sample was …just out of reach.

When John was out of gas money, his shoulders rounded in despair and he simply walked. "Until his last two years, he could walk young men into the ground," Milo's son, John, remembered.

A white man from Tok said of John in those days, "All I ever saw was a bum." He knew nothing of this pioneer, or of his history. Carl Pederson, an old miner and salvage man, said of his friend, John, "I won't talk about a man when he was hurting, when he was down…"

In his 1947 journal, John wrote, "When all at once my star shifted and left me in the shadow, I was alone. The windstorm swept me into the turbulent stream. I fought the high banks, trying to clinch them with my hands. My fingertips were worn. There were no leaning trees, no roots, not even straw floating on the water on either side.

"I could see my friends walking in a park enjoying the scenery, even the turbulent stream.

"Right in front of their eyes, I was struggling for life in the water, but they didn't even see me."

Fred and John

John, smiling on the day of Bob Bloom's visit, c. 1961, in the "Pink Roadhouse"

In 1949, a newcomer, a steam point driller out of Nome by the name of Fred Cook, met John Hajdukovich in Big Delta. John suggested that Fred buy a churn/impact drill for prospecting at Jarvis Creek. Hitting it off, the two of them explored claims in every direction.

"Gold was a not a big thing to 'Uncle' John," Milo's son, John, pointed out. "Coal was more interesting to 'Uncle' John; it had more of a future."

John was full of plans; he was teaching Fred the lay of the land. They intended to prospect along the old telegraph/Goodpaster Trail. However new homesteaders had moved into the area and blocked the old trail. One of them, Pinkerton, wanted private access to his homestead. There had been numerous confrontations. One day, as Fred and John approached in a cat, John, in a semblance of General Patton, stood up and yelled, "HEY! Come and get me, Pinkerton!" Only eighty-four years old, John continued, "You said you wanted to kill me! Now's your chance! Come and get me!!" Young Fred hunkered down in the cat and muttered, "Speak for yourself…"

In the 1963 State of Alaska court trial in which another homesteader challenged the trail's roadblock, John protested, "I'm nice to all the homesteaders. I'm Pinkerton's best friend. Time will prove."

In the years during which John and Fred rambled, John described his life at "Jezero Skadarsko" ['Ye-zeroh Skah-'dar-sko] (Lake Skadar) near Albania in Montenegro. Thirty-six years later, Fred could still perfectly pronounce John's birthplace, rolling the words as a jewel as he remembered John.

"John was better educated than most who came from the Balkans," Fred said. "He spoke several eastern European languages, including Russian and some Arabic."

When John died, the Alaska Pioneers gave him a temporary marker for a gravestone. Fred waited three years for more to be done. Finally, he asked permission, ordered a special grave plaque, and one day, he made a trip to Fairbanks' Birch Hill cemetery.

Fred poured the cement on the grave inset. He left while the concrete set up, but he did not realize that the cemetery kept strict hours. When he returned, the cemetery was locked. There was nothing to do but scale the fence; but in the process, Fred ripped his pants.

However, to his satisfaction, the plaque reading, "John Hajdukovich - A True Alaskan Pioneer" was firmly set "in memoriam."

Even after thirty-seven years, Fred's memories of John remained deeply acute. When asked about this, Fred smiled. "Oh," he murmured, "Maybe...it's because he showed me...where the gold was."

Jack Singleton and C.D. Flannigan

John "Jack" Singleton: Prospector, the Unpaid Teacher of Tetlin, and John's Friend

Jack Singleton came early to the Klondike in 1897 when he was twenty-nine years old. Eleven years older than John, they both cared deeply for the Natives. They were also good friends.

After a Tanana Crossing pastor left in 1918, Singleton volunteered to hold services. His life was one of service. When he moved to Tetlin, he adopted an infant Native son, Teddy. As the boy grew, he needed schooling. John urged Singleton to teach Teddy, as well as the other children. Jack became a father to all: teaching the village children to read, write, do arithmetic, and in the summer, to garden. The mail arrived infrequently, but when it did, Singleton distributed it. When someone was ill, they came to Jack.

The combination of Singleton's care, and the Natives' isolation, rendered the village to be a showcase of purity in the 1930s when inspecting government agents arrived.

Reverend Drane, the itinerant Episcopalian pastor took photographs in 1919, capturing portraits of Teddy, Jack's son, and Tetlin's fragile, fleeting way of life.

John Hajdukovich, c. 83 years old, c. 1962

Changes

Since the gold rush's beginnings, groceries could only be imported by steamboat or barge. But, by 1949, as transportation methods improved, Alaska Freight Lines trucked containerized perishables, delivered fresh from Valdez. The famous green eggs of the Yukon River barge days were over, but yet, some old-timers complained the new eggs…lacked flavor.

C.D. Flannigan

As a very young man, C.D. Flannigan came over the Valdez Trail in 1900 and prospected on the rivers: Tolovana and Kobuk Rivers, following the major gold stampedes. He became a steamboat captain and trader on the Upper Tanana. Known as "Flannigan," he was the only steamboat pilot to complete the difficult

and treacherous trip up the Nabesna river and was one of the few to reach Chisana. He freighted prospectors with the light steamboat, the *Atlas*, named later the *Nabesna*.

As Irish as his beer, Flannigan sold his Nabesna store to Milo Hajdukovich.

One dark night heading down river, Flannigan missed the main river and bottle-necked the *Nabesna* in Hansen Hollow's narrow slough. Ted Lowell

Emil Hammer and Kathleen, Hal and Madge Newton, c. 1924, Healy Lake

said it was rumored Flannigan was slightly intoxicated and that he had done it on purpose. Flannigan's epoch was over and his business had failed.

After this incident, Flannigan got a job at Ladd Field in Fairbanks as a boiler fireman. Known to have been sick for several years, one night in 1950, Flannigan said "Good night" to his wife, stepped into the bedroom and shot himself.

In a few short years, Herman Kessler, Louis Grimsmore, and William Beach, John's wealthy client, were all gone.

Up the river, Chief Walter Northway at Nabesna was struggling with the village's new Native store. With the assistance of the teacher, Pringle, they wrote John twenty letters. They said to each other, "John will help us!"

Jack Singleton, Teddy, David and Mrs. McConnell,
Rev. Francis Drane and dog, Sam, 1919, Tanana Crossing

Transition

Rika closed off half the roadhouse in the 1950s. She and John only needed to heat a small space. John's cabin behind the springhouse was piled high with hunting photos and memoirs. A bakery sign still stood in the brush near the highway, but Rika's clientele was mostly just local fishermen and an occasional soldier.

The roadhouse's bottom logs were rotting. John and Rika got local trapper, John Shulz, to jack up the building to install a

John, trail break, long johns and pack boots, c.1963

"floating floor," but the project drifted…

Rika prevailed on her countryman and dependable carpenter, Louis Grimsmore. She asked her friend to move the frame warehouse, used formerly downstream by the independent truckers during their rebellion. Louis sandwiched the warehouse between his ferryman's cabin and Rika's roadhouse. He converted the truckers' building into Rika's "new roadhouse." She wanted it pink, so Grimsmore obliged her.

In 1953, Rika moved in full of plans: a new roadhouse, a new clientele…

John continued to be gone on his adventures, while Rika maintained their rooms. He busied himself with "the mineral development of the future," and retirement was not in his plans.

Last Hikes

John was an institution and his expertise was frequently needed. Called "The Old Pathfinder," John was tapped by the military and by new pioneers cutting through the Bush.

In the early 1950s, government scientific studies proved that American radar could not protect the country against a nuclear attack. However, the new ultra high frequencies could scour American space. President Eisenhower authorized

3000 miles for a virtual wall of defense across the top of Alaska, Canada, and Greenland: the Distant Early Warning System.

Al Ghezzi of Alaska Freight Lines had secured the contract from the Air Force to freight building materials to the Arctic. John wanted to reconnoiter the road. At his own expense, John hired a small plane. Using his Bush savvy, John questioned trappers about river crossings, glaciation, snow depth, and penciled in a safe route. He recommended the path to Alaska Freight Lines and said they accepted a portion of it. He was paid one month's wages, five hundred dollars, before Ghezzi went bankrupt.

John emphatically observed, "Young Ghezzi is good for the country."

John had lived from steamboats to nuclear threat; from the military's telegraph line to the Distant Early Warning System (the D.E.W. line), stretched across the north. From a country victimized by communism, John was adamant that the D.E.W. line, the arctic sentinel, must be installed.

John, "The Pathfinder" was consulted both for the Alcan's routing, and for settling Tetlin Reserve border disputes.

However, when he was seventy-six, John got a little lost on a ten day, cross-country hike with Native friend, Moses Albert. His bones, he wrote, adapted a little slower to sleeping out in the mountain chill.

They took the wrong ridge coming off Mount Harper. After days of wandering, they shot a caribou…But a little like Rip Van Winkle, they left John's rifle on the summit.

John pushed, with a cane, up 60 miles of steep mountains and through swampy drainages. Finally, they wandered into Healy Lake.

Again, at the age of eighty-two, John flew, in 1961, to the head of the Goodpaster River. After a night of sleeping out, he wrote, "Spread out my sleeping bag and for the first time in forty-seven years, I slept at 5400 feet. It snowed some in the morning."

The next day, as he prospected with wet gloves, his fingers stung with the piercing wind. He commented later, "Tips of my fingers got nipped. Probably this old hide of mine got worn out. Can't take it anymore."

Milo's son, John, said, "Once, a grizzly bear surprised Uncle John, took a swipe at him, and sent him flying to the bottom of the hill!" Shaking his head laughing, young John said, "Uncle John just got up and kept going."

He added, "At seventy-one, John was so tough, he could still outrun his dogs…!"

Maybe one reason John was so fit, according to Ted Lowell was, "John didn't eat nothin'."

When John was interviewed in 1955, Maureen Bauer of the *Fairbanks Daily News-Miner* wrote, "Veteran Trader Still Going In High Gear."

"At first glance," she wrote, "the old trader's appearance would fool you. With his lean face and sensitive, dark features, his deep-set eyes and graying moustache, he resembles a violinist more than a man who has spent 51 years prospecting in the Alaskan wilds. His long tapered fingers once played a violin, but now the old violin sits in a dusty corner untouched.

"John first came to the Interior in 1902 after coming through the Sahara and Arabian country. He recalled the '*Cudahy,*' the ship on which he was traveling in Alaska grounded 20 miles from the Native village of Chena.

"When asked if he plans on retiring, John answered, 'Not until I find that streak of gold I've been looking for 51 years.'"

John remembered that in 1930 when he first went Outside, a woman refused to believe that a man could live in Alaska without freezing to death. John asked her to run her hand over his face and hands and discover, 'Alaska is not all ice and snow.'"

Once, when John was older, Fred Demit stumbled across John sitting near his campfire in the Tanacross flats. "What you doin', John?" Fred asked the old trader. "Just enjoyin' the country….," John smiled. Then, turning to Fred's new bride, John smiled approvingly, "You got a good man there,…and even one with a new truck."

As they left, Fred watched John's smoke curling above the trees.

Perhaps John was remembering when he saw his first marten, a 1904 memory he once scribbled on paper.

Apparently, when John first came to the Fairbanks camp, back in 1904, he put his grubstake on a sled. He slipped the sled's tump line, a head harness, over his crown, and then, pulled the sled tethered to his head. He "necked his load," while snowshoeing, to the Bonnifield strike southwest of Fairbanks. On the way, he saw signs in the snow that reminded him of domestic cat tracks.

The next morning, John got up early and seeing small "cats," he guessed they might be marten. He tried to lasso one. He wrote, "My partner asked why I didn't shoot one." [John had a gun] But he said, "I didn't want to kill no animal, but I wanted to catch one on a line, so I followed them around. Every time the marten gets up to the tree, they climbed up and I was left on the ground looking up the tree they climbed. Then, I made another jump for another marten, and that one climbed up and all that was repeated again until they was all up and spitting at me from the tree. That was my experience with marten in Alaska."

Rika's Roadhouse, new "Pink Roadhouse," Art Smith's float plane, "Old Thomas," Kechumstuk Native in grass to front right, c. 1953

"John was a philosopher," Maury Smith, a former *Jensens' Daily* reporter, said just before he died. "John was a different kind of a guy: a gentle soul who said a lot with his eyes. He loved the out-of-doors and that's healthy.

"People in Fairbanks didn't really know him.

"I'll never forget the sight of his dogs running on the sparkling, hard-packed snow ridge from Northway in 1939."

As homesteaders moved into the raw Delta area, John directed the new pioneers to good timber stands and meadows. He showed Dean Cummings, a log home supplier, the Gerstle spruce stands, where he had once harvested to build the Alcan highway.

John loaned his horse tack to Clearwater homesteader, Norm Cosgrove, and told him to cut the wild hay meadows he had once used.

Where, in 1919, John had improved the Clearwater crossing, Norm had built his home. Later, John asked Norm, "Did you find those meadows?" "Yes!" Norm responded. "And, harvested them two times."

John advised Norm not to incorporate into a borough, saying, "You have minerals in the Tanana valley."

123

MiliceAndjeJovova

Djoko and Ljubo Mijac with neighbor, Andje Hajdukovic, John's daughter in Podgor-Utrg, Montenegro, c. 1973

John never found "as much gold as there were rocks in this valley," his 1903 stated prerequisite for returning home, and so, he never returned home. When statehood finally arrived on John's eightieth birthday, Rika offered John the money to go home. He complained, "It wasn't enough…" and refused to go.

A neighbor from his home in Podgor-Utrg, Ivo Jovetic ['Ee-voh 'Yoveh-teech], had also worked in the West, but had returned home. He simply clucked his tongue over a man who had not. When asked, in 2001, in Podgor, Ivo swagged his head emphatically over the name of Jovo Hajdukovic.

As Ivo's black clad wife sat near the home's cook stove, Ivo pronounced John's name as anathema. According to Ivo, Jovo had virtually abandoned his wife, never seen his daughter, and was therefore, no good.

Milica, John's wife, always wore a black headcovering, as did their daughter, Andje. Their names were pronounced as one unit, in one breath: "MiliceAndjeJovova ['Mee-leetzuh'Ahndjeh'Yovohvoh]:" literally, "Milica, Andje of Jovo."

When, in the early 1950s, Montenegrin friend, Vaso Kentura ['Vah-so 'Kentooruh], discovered John's two women living in absolute destitution, he wrote to John. As soon as John heard of them living in the tiny house devoid of any facilities, he borrowed money to send home. With it, the women built a two story addition. They could then step from the upstairs kitchen into a new upstairs bedroom/living room combination. From outside the house, they could access a new animal stall under the added bedroom.

A Hajdukovic cousin in Montenegro bragged that MiliceAndje's new room was used as a social gathering spot. It was the largest room in the village devoid of children.

Many a night, there was singing and storytelling in the room Jovo had contributed.

Over the years, John had watched other people have children. Once, when he saw Vuka Stepovich's husband, Mike, toss their infant into the air, John exclaimed, "Don't do that! That's how my daughter was crippled."

Vuka remembered that one time John leaned over her baby's bassinet and softly said only to himself, "That's how my daughter would've looked..."

All her life, Andje shepherded the village's herd of sheep and goats. Greatly resembling her father, she was a gentle, tiny woman whose dark, expressive eyebrows, warm, gentle smile, and even, strong jaw were her father's.

Deep in John was always the picture of home. He could easily see Milica stepping out of the ivy-covered front door to call Andje, as her eyes swept the austere, rocky mountains. In the morning light, neighbors called news to each other like Arabs crying from their peaks, singing in a plaintive, undulating language.

Far beyond, lay the blue of Lake Skadar.

When Kenny Thomas playfully challenged John to "go back where you came from...!" John smiled thoughtfully and simply said,..."Ah...that country..."

Silas Solomon remembered, "John got lonely."

Vuka Radovic Stepovich,
Fairbanks, c. 1989,
90th birthday

"They had the best of both worlds"

Mary Hansen of Bert and Mary's roadhouse said emphatically, "Rika would have given her eye teeth to marry John. Back then, we all knew they were romantic; it was common knowledge to all of us." When asked if John and Rika were ever romantic, Fred Demit of Tanacross said simply, "They had a very great love. They allowed each other to be what they were. They took care of each other for fifty years."

Kathy Zachgo, a Clearwater homesteader, said, "They talked to each other like two old married people, but they didn't appear to have that relationship."

Local rancher Emily Keaster said, "I thought it was Hans Seppala she liked, ?

Mary Hansen on her
97th birthday, April 27, 2002

fellow Scandinavian. He did ask her to marry him. She simply laughed at him and the poor man never dared ask again."

Many said, "I think they were just very good friends who really understood each other."

An additional puzzle might be why John, after only one year, gave the roadhouse to Rika for back wages. Perhaps John did not care and let Rika take care of what never interested him: running the roadhouse. Local historian Sharon Haney Wright thought that perhaps John gave Rika the roadhouse to protect it from bill collectors.

Harry Hughes, a centenarian in 1999, claimed the roadhouse was once held as collateral by Fairbanks' outfitter, Bob Bloom. In the early 1960s, Hughes and Bloom traveled together to Delta. According to Hughes, Bloom wrote out a "quickclaim deed" and handed it to John. John was as "happy as a calf in clover," relieved to return the roadhouse to Rika. A picture of that visit seemed to affirm John's jubilation.

However, Key Bank retired president, Bill Stroecker, who knew Bloom well said, "That scenario simply would never have happened."

Some have suggested that John took advantage of Rika. When Carl Tweiten heard this claim, he chuckled, "Oh, I don't know. Who took advantage of whom? Rika got the roadhouse!!"

Sometimes John grinned and teased Rika in front of their company saying, "She tricked me out of the roadhouse!"

Rika would shuffle her high laced shoes and protest, "Oh! Yon!!"

John and Rika differed from each other as Northern Europe does from the Balkans. Rika was a farmer and a saver; John was a hunter and a spender. Both required independence and freedom. Fred Demit concluded, "They had the best of both worlds."

Losing Each Other...

John's wife, Milica, was dead in 1964. John, too, was not feeling well. He made one more trip Outside to visit Edward Mallinckrodt. But while he was gone, Rika climbed her stool awkwardly. She lost her balance and her brittle body hit the roadhouse floor.

When John returned, Rika was in the hospital with a broken hip. John seemed to give up, saying, "When they're ninety like Rika, they just don't come out alive."

However, Fred Cook was concerned as well about John's abdominal pain. Fred and Art Smith took John to the hospital for testing. They thought John and Rika would be happy to see each other and wheeled them individually into a waiting room. On seeing John, Rika exclaimed, "What are you doing here?! You're supposed to be home fixing the well!"

John's dark eyebrows furrowed furiously as he waved his expressive hands. He simply grunted, "Bah! Bahhh!"

In 1965, after Rika was able to return home, John agreed to exploratory surgery, a decision the family later regretted. John's body was inundated with cancer, which was only further complicated by the procedure.

A few days later, Maury Smith visited John in the hospital, "You'll be out of here, John, in a few days..." he lied. Uncharacteristically, John only smiled quietly, and said, "I'm not going anywhere..."

One of the last things John wanted his "nephew," John, to have was his treasured map. On the map was John's heritage to leave Milo's son: where the highway might be re-routed. John encouraged his nephew to invest.

Adding, he asked, "You'll take care of the bills, won't you?"

The next day, July 18, 1965, twenty-seven year old John left the hospital alone. The prospector of 1903 was gone.

Still recuperating from her broken hip, Rika missed John's funeral. Later, she did write a report to his daughter, Andje, saying, "Your father, as one of the oldest pioneers, was given a large funeral and one of the best plots in the cemetery."

She added, "He found two honest men who would take care of you after his death. One is Krstun, your cousin in Titograd, who speaks your language, and he will write. When I am better, I will send you your father's photos and letters."

She gently explained to Andje, "Your father was always in my house except when he was in the mountains."

Most likely worried about the estate, she cautioned Andje regarding John's debt, "Don't deal with any lawyers without first consulting me."

(These letters from Rika to Andje were kept in Andje's drawer and remained there for 24 years after her death in 1974).

In 1974, Andje's neighbor, Mijac ['Mee yach], found her lying dead next to the family tree where she had been feeding her chickens. Her body was laid next to her mother's, in their more wealthy relative's vault in the church cemetery, nestled into the mountain. The view was equal to John's on Birch Hill in Fairbanks.

John's estate was valued at two thousand dollars, only a token of the twenty-three thousand dollars he owed his creditors. The life insurance he had retained for his daughter never found its way to Yugoslavia.

A Butterfly

Setting out one day in 1999 to find John's grave, this author felt that there was no doubt it would be on the summit of Birch Hill in the sunshine. There it was, next to a solitary tree.

Flying with the sunlight reflecting through its wings, a yellow butterfly did peaceful loop the loops, landed on a lilac bush near John's grave, and then, on an evergreen tree.

Rika

Rika and Bill Crisler, c.1965, Fort Greely, Delta Junction, Alaska

Rika spent a lot of time looking out the window as she healed in the pink roadhouse. One of her visitors was Milo's son, John. Young John asked if he might take his uncle's records to submit to the University of Alaska's archives. Rika said emphatically, "No" and moved all the memorabilia into the pink roadhouse.

Five months after John was gone, when Rika was ninety years old , a neighbor, Art Smith, loaded her wood stove twice a day, during the winter of 1965. Rika was still using a walker and was frail. At -50° F., Christmas Eve night, a fire exploded in the chimney. Rika, having mere minutes, and wearing only a light housecoat, crawled from her walker outside.

She was terrified that she might be overlooked in the dark. Determined, she pulled herself up using the outside mirror of her car, but the cold metal froze her fingers. Incredibly, she held on for fifteen minutes, until finally her neighbors, the Pinkertons, happened to drive by.

Rika was taken to Fort Greely (Allen Army Airfield, five miles south of Delta Junction) by ambulance where she was diagnosed with first and second degree frostbite.

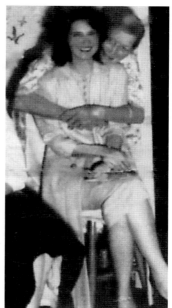

Nothing, however, remained of the pink house. Fifty years of John's records, Rika's gold, money, native costume, and weavings — all were gone. Only the concrete stairs, a cake tin of John's journals, and the ruined safe remained.

Rika convalesced with various families, including young John and his wife, Marcia Hajdukovich. After she was able to once again feed herself, Rika began living with the Bill Zachgo family in Delta.

Rika and Pat Theisen,
Delta Homemakers' Club;
Rika's birthday c. 1967

"Rika needed full-time care," Kathy Zachgo remembered. "But she refused to live in the Pioneer Home, principally because she thought it cost too much. More importantly, she didn't want to lose her independence.

"She had no business living alone, but we'd done all we could and she insisted on returning to the little 'ferryman's cabin' rather than go to the Pioneer's Home."

Small and hard, Rika, at age ninety, kept plunging her own laundry into heated water on her wood, cook stove. She slept without a mattress and used a Hudson's Bay blanket for her coverlet.

But, her home was surrounded by a deep bed of orange Tiger Lilies.

Rika's already thick Swedish accent was intensified by her loose, false teeth. She told Judy Pease, her friend, "I yust sit and s(h)it vaiting for sumvun to wisit."

If anyone wanted to fish near the roadhouse, it was understood that they first had tea with Rika, served hot in her Swedish pink copper kettle.

The local Larrabee family fished a lot. As soon as Rika heard their outboard, she heated oil in her skillet for the expected fish.

Though she rarely socialized with other women, her birthday was celebrated in 1967 by the Delta Homemakers' Club.

But Rika's heart was weakening. In the spring of 1969, at age ninety-four, Rika was found by a neighbor, dead from pulmonary edema.

Rika was buried in the grove of birch trees on the knoll near Wallen Airfield, south of the roadhouse. Rika was known on both sides of the Atlantic for her extreme thrift. Perhaps her most lavish investment was her life-long friendship with John Hajdukovich.

While John slept quietly on the hill above Fairbanks, Rika was, in 1998, near the bustling crowds of the new state park, Rika's Roadhouse. One hundred years after the Klondike gold rush of 1898, a centennial flag hung from the roadhouse door. A tour guide was explaining "John was never home, while Rika..." when suddenly she was interrupted by someone in the crowd. She paused, slightly irritated. A driver's license was being thrust into the face of the tour guide. In the lamplight, she slowly read, "John...Haj...du...ko...vich," and...looked up incredulously to see a man with brown, twinkling eyes.

Grinning in broad Montenegrin style, Milo's son, John, was back in the roadhouse. Wearing his cousin's wide-brimmed hat, he easily impersonated the generous prospector from Podgor-Utrg.

Epilogue: Surviving Family in Sweden and Montenegro

Branko Hajdukovic, Podgor-Utrg, Montenegro, 2001

Neither Rika nor John has any direct descendants. John's cousins still comprise half of his home village of Podgor Utrg, Montenegro, formerly known as the Federal Republic of Yugoslavia. Milo's nephew, Branko Hajdukovic, and his niece, Danica Hajdukovic, live in Bijelo Polje ['Beyel-uh 'Pohl-yuh] and Podgorica ['Pohd goreetza], Montenegro. Two distant, but very supportive cousins, Anica Hajdukovic of Belgrade and Dr. Dragan Hajdukovic of Geneva, Switzerland have contributed invaluable research time and materials to this account. None of the Balkan Hajdukovics have, as yet, been able to travel to Alaska due to ten years of wars, bombing, and sanctions. When I, as the first representative of Jovo, arrived in 1998 in Podgor, Ilinka Hajdukovic wept, embracing me saying, "Finally someone came…" Ilinka had been a caring daughter to Andje.

Tabessa John, Tetlin elder, 1998

Two sets of Rika's relatives from her hometown, Orebro, as well as from Goteborg, have visited the roadhouse: Roland Thorstensson, Rigmor Ohman, and her sister, Margrethe.

In 1998, in John's old house in Podgor Utrg, young Jelena Mijach found the letters from Rika and John to Andje in John's daughter, Andje's, desk, standing in the middle of a rotten floor. Not able to speak English, but knowing what I wanted, Jelena leapt across a second story, rain-sodden platform to thrust her hand into the desk's drawer and retrieve the letters from Big Delta.

Today, Djoko Mijach ['Djoh-koh 'Mee-yach] stores

Gunn-Britt Andersson, Rika's niece, Solna, Sweden, 1998

131

grain where Andje once kept her goats. John's neighbors, the Ljubo ['Lyoo-boh] Mijach family, who took care of Milica Andje, still guard over the house.

Anyone interested in restoring John's home in Montenegro should contact this author or Branko Hajdukovic of Bijelo Polje.

A life-link has now been permanently established between Yugoslavia, Sweden, and Alaska.

Extraordinarily, the name "Hajduk" resounds on both sides of the Atlantic. Alaska's Interior "Hajduks" echo the ancient name, "Hajduk," from the rugged mountains of Montenegro. Mount Hajdukovich in Alaska is a landmark to Natives and whites alike. In the Great Land, ours is a parallel destiny.

MAP OF
ALASKA
SCALE

Hajdukovich's Alaska, Landmarks
Of the Big Delta Region

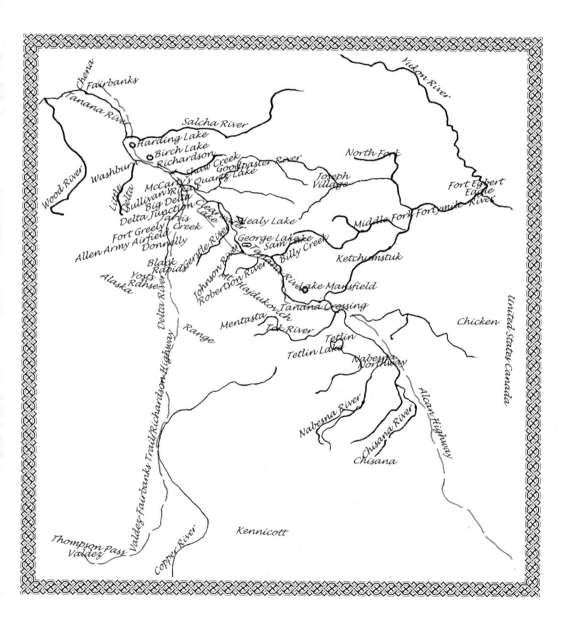

TRADERS IN THE LATE 1920S-EARLY 1930S

Emil Hammer at Healy
C. D. Flannigan at Tetlin
Herman Kessler at Nabesna
Ole Fredrickson at Tanana Crossing
John Hajdukovich at Tanana Crossing, Tetlin and Nabesna
Milo Hajdukovich also in Tanana Crossing, Tetlin and Nabesna between 1922-32

Poling Boats vs. Outboards

Before motors: 29 days poling McCarty to Nabesna.
In 1928, with an outboard: 200 miles upstream in 51 hours. Return trip downstream: 12 hours.

Old and New Vehicular Traffic on the Valdez-Fairbanks Trail - Average per year

1902 - c. 1923: 30 wagons and 24 sleds.
1923 on: 817 motor vehicles on "Richardson Highway;" roadhouses increased their overnight accommodation.

Boats

John's Boats: John's launch was 40 feet with a 25/35 h.p. outboard. A tug accompanied the launch.
Milo's Boat: a 75 h.p. motor on a grey, 40 foot boat.
Freight costs: $0.125 per pound up the river and $0.10 per pound down.

Amounts of Freight Hauled

1929: First, by truck from Fairbanks to McCarty/Big Delta: 150-200 tons of merchandise. Then, traders freighted up-river by gas boat to Hammer's, Hajdukoviches', Kessler's, Ole Fredrickson's and Flannigan's trading posts.

Mail

Roy Lund delivered mail by dogs, double enders or truck twice a month.

Standard Report on Grundler-Tanana Crossing Trail.

To Hawley W. Sterling, Supertendent-From Frank Nash, Alaska Road Commission Supervisor, March 10th, 1928

Cabins - Shelters Along the Trail

Big Delta/Grundler to Clearwater:
12 miles. 6 by 6 foot tent of an Indian trapper's.

Roadhouses at both Grundler/McCarty and at Clearwater.

Clearwater to Healy:
24 miles to Emil Hammer's trading post;
they were poor, extra cabins.

Healy to Eight Mile point: 8 miles.
John Hajdukovich has a cabin 1 mile up.
Chief Joe has one, both are kept locked.
Two more cabins are further up:"If you don't know where the key is cached, you're out of luck."
Six miles further, there is an Indian tent.

Eight miles to Little Gerstle River:
14 miles to Hugh Ross' cabin.
(On the opposite side of the river, there is an open cabin.)

Little Gerstle to George Lake:
3 native cabins. One is John Hajdukovich's, 6 miles left side of George Creek.

George Lake to Sam Creek: 16 miles.

Sam Creek to 3 cabins: 17 miles.

3 Cabins to Paul's Cabin: 3 miles.
Seven native cabins, one is Hajdukovich's.

Paul's Cabin to Jimmy cabin: 10 miles, very steep.

Jimmy's Cabin to Tanana Crossing: 14 miles.
8 miles further, there is a trapper's tent.
There are several native cabins.
John Hajdukovich has two cabins. There is no roadhouse.

Credits

Articles published in "Rika's Remembered" series, Fairbanks Daily News-Miner, 1998, and their individual credits:

"Opening the Deep Freeze," May 10, 1998: *An Expedition to The Copper, Tanana, Koyukuk Rivers in 1885* by Lieutenant Henry T. Allen; *The Opening of Alaska* by Brig. Gen. William L. "Billy" Mitchell; Ltn. Joseph C. Castner, *Castner's Expedition; Valdez Trail;* and Bill Stroecker.

"Leaving the Old Country," May 24, 1998: Dr. Miroslav Konstantinovic, Belgrade; Marie Esplund-Lynn, archivist in Orebro, Sweden; Orebro recording office, Orebro, Sweden; Kitty Wisner, Church of Jesus Christ of Latter-day Saints researcher, Utah; Rika's Roadhouse/Big Delta State Historical Park.

"Trails, Telegraphs, Trading Posts Pave Way," June 7, 1998.

"Hajduk Comes into the High Country," June 28, 1998: The following are acknowledged for their assistance in researching this article: the Rex Fisher Collection, *"Liars and Thieves: Alonzo Maxey and the U.S. Army Signal Corps"* by Stephanie Stirling, Vuka Stepovich, *Alaska, Big Delta and the Goodpaster Region* by Carl Tweiten, Irene Mead, Paul Solka, Fred Cook; *Alaska Roadhouses* by Walter Phillips, Meta Bloom.

"Search For An Elusive Pot of Gold," July 12, 1998: The following are acknowledged for assistance in researching this article: Rika's Roadhouse, *"WAMCATS: McCarty Military Reserve,"* Alaska Department of Natural Resources, Division of Parks, Office of History and Archeology; Fred Cook; *Born With the River* by Craig Mishler; Rex Fisher Collection; Charles Michael Brown Collection; *Shushanna: Alaska's Last Great Gold Rush* by Mark Kirchhoff; *Alaska Roadhouses* by Walter Phillips; Irene Mead; Lael Hibschman; Vuka Stepovich; University of Alaska Archives/Hajdukovich Collection, Box 5, Item 219; John Hajdukovich Sr.; Harrie Hughes; and Evolyn Melville.

"Rika Makes Home Away From Home," July 26, 1998: Fred John; Mary Hansen; Enna Albert; Tim Luke; State of Alaska interview Ted Lowell; Judy Pease

"John, Rika Build Their Reputations," August 9, 1998: Gunn-Britt Andersson of Solna, Sweden; Roland Thorstensson of Vintrosa, Sweden; Rex Fisher, Fairbanks; Florence Holmes, Fairbanks; Irene Mead, Delta; Bob Redding, Washington; John Hajdukovich, Fairbanks; Doug Christopherson, Delta; Carl Tweiten; Bradford Endicott; Charles Michael Brown's collection and *Indians, Traders and Bureaucrats in the Upper Tanana District: A History of the Tetlin Reserve;* Candace Waugaman's *"Alaska, The Richardson Road;"* State of Alaska, Division of Parks, Rika's Roadhouse interviews; Wendell Endicott's *Adventures in Alaska and Along the Trail;* University of Alaska *Fairbanks Daily News-Miner* archives: September 15-16 1919, April 16-19, 1920.

"Generosity Was Way of the Frontier," August 23, 1998: Charles Michael Brown's collection and *Indians, Traders and Bureaucrats in the Upper Tanana District: A History of the Tetlin Reserve;* University of Alaska archives, John Hajdukovich collection, Box 5, Item 219; Wendell Endicott's *Adventure in Alaska and Along the Trail;* Bradford Endicott, Boston; Kenny Thomas, Tanacross; Tanacross Tribal Council President, Jerry Isaac; Fred Demit, Tanacross; Tetlin council vice president, Larry Mark; Bernie Paul, Village Security Police; Alfred John, Tetlin; George Simpanen, Fairbanks; Cal White, Fairbanks.

"Becoming People of the New Country," September 6, 1998: Alaska Linck, Fairbanks; Oscar Tweiten, Fairbanks; Carl Tweiten, Washington; Paul Kirsteatter, Healy Lake; Maury Smith, Washington; Martha Isaac, Tanacross; Kenny Thomas, Tanacross; Vuka Stepovich, Fairbanks; Dr. Miroslav Konstantinovic, Belgrade; Gunn-Britt Andersson, Solna, Sweden; State of Alaska, Division of Parks; "Big Delta" by Stephanie Stirling; Rika's Roadhouse taped interviews; University of Alaska archives.

"Roadhouse Owner Did It Her Way," September 27, 1998: Dick Osborne, Washington; Florence Holmes, Fairbanks; Bob Redding, Washington; Gene Rogge, Fairbanks; Mary Hansen, Delta.

"Swapping the Wilderness For the Alcan," October 4, 1998: Tanacross Council President, Jerry Isaac; Mary Gene, Tetlin; *Alaska, A History of the 49th State* by Claus M. Naske and Herman E. Slotnick; Irene Mead's *"Life in Big Delta/the Construction of the Alcan;"* John Hajdukovich collection, Box 5, Item 219.

"Hajdukovich Trail Leads to Montenegro," October 18, 1998: Branko and Aleksandra Hajdukovic, Bijelo Polje, Montenegro, FRY; Dr. Dragan Hajdukovic, Geneva, Switzerland; Danica Hajdukovic, Podgorica, Montenegro, FRY; Jovan and Ilinka Hajdukovic, Podgor-Utrg, Montenegro, FRY; Ljubo and Jelena Mijach, Podgor-Utrg, Montenegro, FRY.

"More Light From A Swedish Window," November 1, 1998: Rika's brother, Jakob's, son, John Jakobsson; Rika's sister, Carolina Eriksson's, daughter, Agnes Andersson's, grandchildren: Gunn-Britt Andersson, Roland Thorstensson, Britta Gellert, Bengt Eriksson and Agnes' great granddaughters, Rigmor Olman; Fred Cook, Delta.

"A Family Left Behind, A Dream Out of Reach," November 15, 1998: Branko and Aleksandra Hajdukovic, Bijelo Polje, Montenegro, FRY; Dr. Dragan Hajdukovic, Geneva, Switzerland; Danica Hajdukovic, Podgorica, Montenegro; Jovan and Ilinka Hajdukovic, Podgor-Utrg, Montenegro, FRY; Ljubo and Jelena Mijach, Podgor-Utrg, Montenegro, FRY; Aleksandar Berkuljan, King's Palace curator, Cetinje, Montenegro, FRY; University of Alaska, John Hajdukovich collection, Box 5, Item 219.

"Did He Know Where the Gold Was?" November 29, 1998: State of Alaska Court System; 1963 "Pinkerton vs. Yates;" Fred Cook, Delta.

"Old-Timers Leave Delta Inheritance," December 6, 1998: Norman and Lois Cosgrove, Dean Cummings, Mary Lou Larrabee, James Harrild, Irene Mead, Sharon Haney Wright, Delta; John Hajdukovich, Fairbanks; Paul Kirsteatter, Healy Lake; Charlie and Helen David, Tetlin; Attorney Edward Niewohner, Fairbanks.

"Last Days Of the Delta Old-Timers," December 13, 1998: Mihailo Hajdukovic, Podgorica, Montenegro, FRY; Harrie Hughes, Circle Hot Springs, Alaska; Lois Cosgrove/Delta Gazette, December 29th, 1965 editor Jane Pender; Betty Smith, Fairbanks.

"Holiday Traditions, Pioneer History," December 20, 1998: Mary Hajdukovich Hollander, Fairbanks; Sven-Christer Ohman, Goteborg, Sweden; Branko and Jovan Hajdukovich, Montenegro, FRY.

Letters between John and Andje; between Rika and Andje:
courtesy of Dr. Dragan and Branko Hajdukovic, Serbia-Montenegro.
Translators of all Serbian documents:Blazo Sredanovic, Montenegrin American
Association, Menlo Park, California, Dr. Miroslav Konstantinovic, Dr. Dragan Hajdukovic.
Kathleen Newton Shafer, Lee Saylor and Jeannie Healy, Paul Kirsteatter, Healy Lake

List of Inside Illustrations

Glossary/Pronunciation Guide

Aleuts (*Aleut*) ['Al-ee-oots] - non-Athabaskan Natives of Alaska who live on the Aleutian chain of islands.

Aniak (*Athabaskan*) ['An-ee-ak] - an Alaskan village where Sam Voich lived.

Andjelina or **Andje Hajdukovic** (*Serbian*) ['Ahnd-juh-lee-na] or ['Ahnd-jeh 'Hi-doo-koh-vich] - John Hajdukovich's daughter. She was born after he left Yugoslavia. Andje means "angel."

Batzulnetas (*Athabaskan*) ['Baht-zool-netuz] - an Athabaskan village at the start of the primary trade route leading north across the Alaska Range.

Bijelo Polje (*Serbian*) ['Beyel-uh 'Pohl-yuh] - a town in Montenegro, Yugoslavia where some of Milo Hajdukovich's relatives currently live.

Cetinje (*Serbian*) ['Sehteen-yeh] - original Montenegrin capital city.

Ch'in Chedl Chen (*Athabaskan*) [Chin 'Ch-dl 'Ch-n] - Athabaskan settlement near George Lake.

Crna Gora (*Serbian*) ['Sir-nuh 'Gor-uh] - the Serbian name for Montenegro.

Crnojevic Rijeka (*Serbian*) ['Sirnoye-vich 'Ree-yekuh] - a river valley near John Hajdukovich's home in Montenegro, Yugoslavia.

Djoko Mijach (*Serbian*) ['Djoh-koh 'Mee-yach] - a neighbor of the Hajdukovic's in Podgor-Utrg who currently stores grain where Andje Hajdukovic once kept her goats.

Geti Thege (*Athabaskan*) ['Gh-tee 'Th-eg] - Athabaskan name of Chief Healy's father.

gusle (*Serbian*) ['goose-lay] - a one-stringed Serbian instrument played by sawing the string with the instrument braced against a person's knee.

Hajdukovic (*Serbian*) ['Hi-doo-koh-vich] - John Hajdukovich's original sir name.

Hajduks (*Serbian*) ['Hi-dooks] - Hajduk was not originally a name, but a vocation, that of being a soldier, an "anti-Turkish highwayman." Because "Hajduk" was not originally a name, but a vocation, Jovo's root family name was not Hajdukovich, but Strahinjicha [Straheenneechah] (the possessive form of the name).

Ilija Milajic (*Serbian*) ['Ee-leeyah 'Meelye-eech] - Milo and John's friend, later known as "Charlie Miller."

Ivo Jovetic (*Serbian*) ['Ee-voh 'Yoveh-teech] - a neighbor of John's in Podgor-Utrg, who worked in the West for a time, but returned to Montenegro.

Jelena Lesperovic (*Serbian*) ['Yel-enuh 'Lespehr-vich] - maiden name of Milo Hajdukovich's wife.

Jezero Skadarsko (*Serbian*) ['Ye-zeroh 'Skahdar-sko] - Serbian name for Lake Skadar, a lake in Montenegro near Albania.

Jokana Hajdukovic (*Serbian*) [Yoh-'kan-uh 'Hi-doo-koh-vich] - John Hajdukovich's mother.

Jovo Hajdukovic (*Serbian*) ['Yo-voh 'Hi-doo-koh-vich] - John Hajdukovich's birthname.

Jovovo (*Serbian*) ['Yo-vovoh] - Literally: belonging to John. In the Montenegrin understanding, the term applied to John Hajdukovich's wife and daughter.

kafana (*Serbian*) [kuh-'fah-na] - a Montenegrin bar where men's business was transacted.

Kechumstuk [Ketchumstuck] - U.S. military telegraph station.

Kolasin (*Serbian*) ['Koh-lasheen] - a village in Montenegro, Yugoslavia. Original home of Milo Hajdukovic, John's cousin.

Korzo (*Serbian*) ['Kor-zoh] - the special promenade in Montenegro, Yugoslavia, when young men and women parade up and down the street visiting each other.

Kotor (*Serbian*) ['Koh-tohr] - means "Key." It is a medieval, walled city in Montenegro, Yugoslavia. A look-out church was built high in the mountain above the city, a sentinel overlooking the Bay of Kotor, Montenegro's mouth into the Adriatic Sea.

Krsto Hajdukovic (*Serbian*) [Kirsto 'Hi-doo-koh-vich] - John Hajdukovich's father.

Lesperovic (*Serbian*) ['Lespehr-vich] - Jovan Lesperovic was an old friend of Milo Hajdukovich's, and the father of Milo's wife, Jelena.

Lovcen (*Serbian*) ['Lohv-chen] - Montenegro's sentinel mountain near the city of Cetinje.

Ljubica (*Serbian*) ['Loo-beet-za] - the given name of one of Milo Hajdukovich's sisters.

Ljubo Mijach (*Serbian*) ['Lyoo-boh 'Mee-yach] - a neighbor of the Hajdukovic's in Podgor-Utrg who continues to guard over the house where John, Milica and Andje Hajdukovic once lived.

Maja Stina (*Swedish*) [Mahja Stinuh] - Rika Wallen's mother's maiden name.

Mendaes Chaege Menn (*Athabaskan*) [Mindez 'Ch-gh Min] - original name of Healy Lake.

Mihailovich (*Serbian*) [Mee-'hy-loh-vich] - Pete Mihailovich, a friend of John's, who lived in Napaimute, Alaska.

Mihaljevic (*Serbian*) [Mee-'hal-je-vich] - Nikola Mihaljevic known as "Nick Mellick."

Mijac (*Serbian*) ['Mee-yach] - a Montenegrin neighbor who found Andje Hajdukovic dead.

MiliceAndjeJovova (*Serbian*) ['Mee-leetzuhAhndjeh] - the names of John Hajdukovich's wife and daughter run together and pronounced in Montenegro as if they were one organism, not two people. Literally, "Milica, Andje of Jovo."

Milica Vukmanovic (*Serbian*) ['Mee-leetzuh 'Vook-mah-noh-vich] - John Hajdukovich's wife's name. Milica means "sweet one."

Napaimute (*Athabaskan*) [Nuh-'pie-myut] - an Alaskan village where Pete Mihailovich lived.

Na teyDeh (*Athabaskan*) ['Nah 't-deh] - means: chips exploding from a burst rock. Name given to twin brothers in Athabaskan story.

Niktza Hajduka Strahinjicha (*Serbian*) [Neektzuh 'Hi-dookuh Straheenneechah] - Niktza was the patriarch of the Strahinijic family. Some of the family decided to call themselves "Hajdukovic" and drop the sir name of Strahinijic, while the other faction of the family retained the name. Today, living in the same expanded family house in Podgor-Utrg, there are both Hajdukovics and Strahinijics.

Orebro (*Swedish*) [Ooruh-'broo] - town in Sweden southeast of Sodra Walla, the Jakobsson estate.

Podgorica (*Serbian*) ['Pohd-goreetza] - a town in Montenegro, Yugoslavia where some of Milo Hajdukovich's relatives currently live.

Podgor-Utrg (*Serbian*) [Poh-'dgor Oo-'turg] - the village in Montenegro, Yugoslavia where John Hajdukovich was born and lived until he was 25. "Podgor" means "lying at the base of the mountains:" the piedmont area.

Rade (*Serbian*) ['Rah-day] - John Hajdukovich's cousin, an Orthodox priest, he was a consulate in the court of the Montenegrin king, King Nikola.

Salchaket (*Athabaskan*) ['Sahl-shaket] - an Athabaskan village.

Skadar (*Serbian*) [Skuh-'dar] - a lake near John Hajdukovich's home in Montenegro, Yugoslavia. Jezero Skadarsko is the name of the lake in Serbian. Skadar is the largest inland body of water in the Balkans.

Sodra Walla (*Swedish*) ['Soo-druh 'Val-uh] - Rika Wallen's father, Jakob Jakobsson's, estate in Sweden.

Strahinjicha (*Serbian*) [Straheenneechah] - The original sir name of the "Hajdukovics." See "Niktza Hajduka Strahinjicha" for further explanation.

T'aaiy Ta' (*Athabaskan*) [Tah-ee 'tuh] - the original, Athabaskan name of Chief Northway.

Tysslingen (*Swedish*) [Tissleengih] - a lake in Sweden near the Jakobsson estate of Sodra Walla.

Utashe (*Serbian*) [Oo-'stah-shee] - Croatian nationalists/Axis sympathizers during World War II.

uzma (*Serbian*) ['oozmuh] - a person who is mentally and physically deficient.

Vaso Kentura (*Serbian*) ['Vah-so 'Ken-tooruh] - a friend in Montenegro who wrote to John telling him that John's wife and daughter were destitute.

verige (*Serbian*) ['vehr-eejg] - a Montenegrin hearth/a suspended pot above the cooking fire.

Virpazar (*Serbian*) ['Veer-puhzahr] - a town in Montenegro, Yugoslavia near John's home of Podgor-Utrg.

Voich (*Serbian*) ['Voy-eech] - Sam Voich, a friend of John's, who lived in Aniak.

Vukmanovic (*Serbian*) ['Vook-mah-noh-vich] - John's wife, Milica's, maiden name. Vukmanovic and Hajdukovic are the two largest families in Podgor-Utrg, Montenegro, Yugoslavia.

Ziveli! (*Serbian*) [Zheevuhlee!] - To life!

ᎮᏯ ᏟᏗ

Note from the author:

We welcome any response to **Parallel Destinies, An Alaskan Odyssey.**
Your in-put is valuable. I may be reached (internationally: 99) 1-907 895 4101;
by email: outpost@wildak.net;
by mail at Box 130, Delta Junction, Alaska 99737 USA.
Website: http://www.alaska-highway.org/deltanewsweb/archives/judy_ferguson.htm

Parallel Destinies, An Alaskan Odyssey,
may be ordered through Glas Publishing: 1-907 895 4101;
email: outpost@wildak.net;
mailing address: Box 130, Delta Junction, Alaska 99737 USA.
Thank you for your interest, your support in
Parallel Destinies, An Alaskan Odyssey.
We want to hear what you have to say.
Glas, in Serbian, means Voice.
All men have something to say.

Thank you.
Judy Ferguson